D1270925

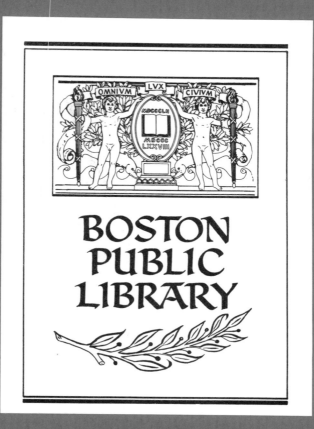

THE HUNGER ROAD

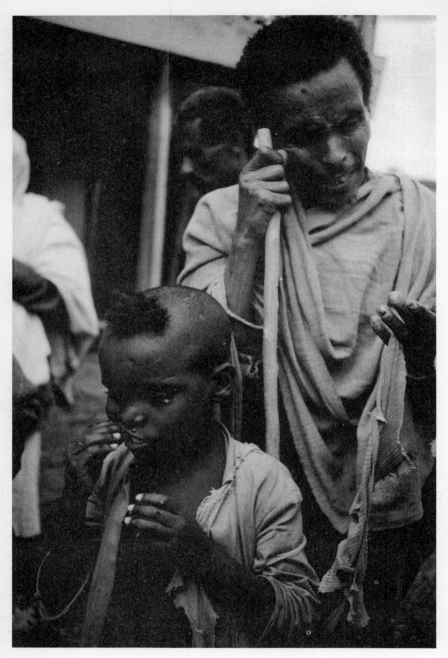

Refugees awaiting food distribution in Ethiopia.

THE
HUNGER
ROAD

Refugees awaiting food distribution in Ethiopia.

THE HUNGER ROAD

JOHN CHRISTOPHER FINE

ATHENEUM   1988   NEW YORK

Books by John Christopher Fine

Sunken Ships and Treasure

Oceans in Peril

The Hunger Road

Atheneum
Macmillan Publishing Company
866 Third Avenue, New York, NY 10022
Collier Macmillan Canada, Inc.
First Edition
Printed in U.S.A.

Library of Congress Cataloging-in-Publication Data
Fine, John Christopher.
The hunger road/by John Christopher Fine.—1st ed.
p.   cm.
Bibliography: p.
Includes index.
Summary: Discusses world starvation, its escalation because of
poverty and inequities in distributing a limited food supply, and
past and present efforts to alleviate the problem.
ISBN 0-689-31361-6
1. Poor—Juvenile literature. 2. Starvation—Juvenile literature.
3. Food relief—Juvenile literature. 4. Food supply—Juvenile literature. [1. Starvation. 2.
Food relief. 3. Food supply.
4. Poor.] I. Title.
HC79.P6F56 1988
363.8—dc19
87-27794 CIP AC

Dedicated to
Monsignor Robert Charlebois
A friend of the poor, an enemy of bureaucracy, and a
servant of God. As a director of Catholic Relief Services'
Eurasia Programs, his work made a difference.
Father Bob insists that caring for the hungry
is not charity, it is justice.
One word describes his dedication, this dedication: LOVE.

Snatched from the jaws of death, but only for a while. Monsignor Robert Charlebois at Neak Luong, Cambodia, where Catholic Relief Services tried to cope with refugees who came sick and starving into enclaves defended by government soldiers. Shortly after this photograph was taken, Neak Luong fell and reports of atrocity and terror sealed the fate of this little child and thousands of others.

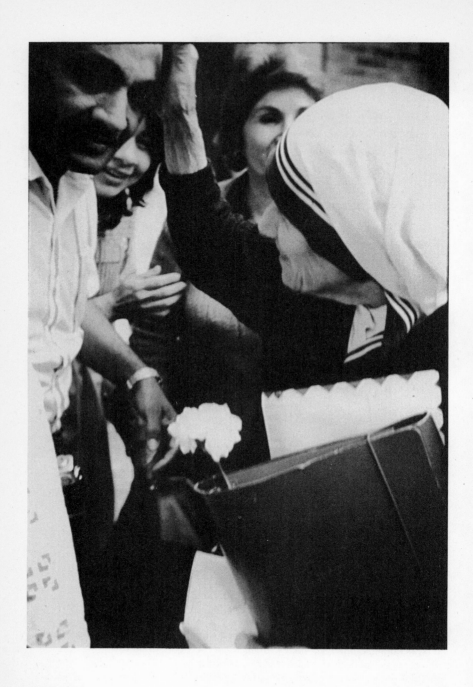

Mother Teresa

A Special Message from Mother Teresa

They serve the poorest of the poor. They care for abandoned children. They bring the dying in from the gutters and streets of Calcutta, India, where they were left homeless, unloved, and uncared for to suffer their last days and hours alone. Mother Teresa and the Catholic Sisters of the Missionaries of Charity live their religion each day in service to others.

For Mother Teresa the real plight of the homeless in the world is not the absence of material things. "Homelessness is not for want of bricks, it is being unwanted, unloved," Mother Teresa says.

Mother Teresa often tells stories about people who have found true happiness helping others, like the young couple who were just married in India. "These two young people came to me and gave me some money," Mother Teresa recounts. "Where did you get so much money? I asked them."

"We decided to get married and we decided not to buy any clothes or gifts but to give the money to you for your work," the young people answered.

"But in our country, India, that is not done. Having good clothes and property at marriage is an important thing," Mother Teresa countered, studying the young couple.

The couple answered, "But, Mother, we love each other so much that we decided we do not need the clothes or gifts. We decided to give it to you for the people you serve."

In the next moment Mother Teresa said what is central to her life's work and belief: "The fruit of love is service—the fruit of service is peace."

Mother Teresa's abounding love, her life of caring for the dying, the sick and abandoned, transcends the artificial boundaries and distinctions some people put up around religions. These Catholic Sisters minister to Hindus, to Moslems, to any and all faiths, and to those without any profession of faith. Their love is a universal truth, an example of human compassion and understanding.

I asked Mother Teresa to write a message expressing that love for this book. Taking up my pen in her large, strong hands, she looked up at me, touched my arm and hand, then wrote this message for you, which is not only an expression of her own strong faith but is the essence of her being; a universal truth for all people about caring.

Love one another
as Jesus loves
each one of you
God bless you
M Teresa mc

CONTENTS

Food being distributed to refugees in Ethiopia.

Preface

Along the road they come . . . frail waifs, skeletal bodies protruding from the tatters that hang from fleshless shoulders. They have come starving from the country. They have come to the road searching for help. Along the way many have died, obscurely in the bush, on the tracks and jungle paths, upon the desert, and in the little villages where once they lived. Many are dead already, just dying slowly.

It is the same everywhere. In the end, if they can, they come to the road to die. It is not one road, but every track and tarmac that leads through civilization, to someplace where they've heard there's hope. Any who have once seen it—streaming humanity, the procession of refugees with no way back and only uncertainty ahead—will recognize starvation's transient address: It is called the Hunger Road.

John Christopher Fine

INTRODUCTION:
Obesity and Starvation

"Ton of Trouble: Fat Kids on Rise," read the recent headline of a major New York City newspaper. The article, describing the problems of overweight young people in the United States, stated: "Obesity among American kids has increased more than 50 percent in two decades, and the nation is facing an epidemic of childhood weight problems." The article also reported on a study conducted by the Harvard School of Public Health, which found that nearly a third of all American preteen white males are overweight, that there has been a 54 percent increase in obesity among six to eleven year olds and a 36 percent increase in obesity among young people aged twelve to seventeen.

The Harvard study is not unique. The Washington University School of Medicine in St. Louis, Missouri, has just published its findings that "In America, land of plenty, 34 million Americans are obese. Four in twenty women and three in twenty men tip the scales at least 100 pounds more than they should."

Contrast these statistics with the United Nations Children's Fund (UNICEF) report, *The State of the World's Children*, which says, "By far the greatest emergency facing the world's children today is the 'silent emergency' of frequent infection and widespread undernutrition—an emergency which kills well over a quarter of a million children *every week.*"

The World Food Council currently reports that one billion people in the world are hungry, "chronically undernourished." Every year 13 to 18 million people die from starvation. Each day, every twenty-four hours, 35,000 people on our planet die from starvation; twenty-

1

We can plant the land and farm and fish the sea, but overuse and abuse of land resources and dependence on chemical fertilizers, herbicides, pesticides, and insecticides have caused grave consequences to the long term environmental picture. Of the 13 billion hectares of land on Earth, only about 3.2 billion hectares can be used to cultivate food. It is estimated that 1.4 billion hectares are presently being used to raise food to feed the world population.

four people starve to death every minute. Eighteen of those twenty-four are children under five years of age, human beings who have suffered and died even before they have begun to live.

The statistics about starvation and hunger are grim. When contrasted with reports and statistics showing gluttony, greed, avarice, indifference, corruption, and cruelty, it leaves us with a rather bleak impression of human conscience.

Of the 13 billion hectares (a hectare is 10,000 square meters of area, or 2.471 acres) of land on Earth, only about 3.2 billion hectares can be used to cultivate food. An estimated 1.4 billion hectares of land are presently being cultivated to raise food to feed the world population. From all that we see around us, we know that we are fast depleting these limited land resources. As humankind turns toward the ocean resources, we find that pollution, greed, and abuse have also limited their potential to supply food for a current world population of about 5 billion people. Today's population is 3 billion more than the world population in 1930, and economists predict that forty years from now, the world population will rise to about 8.2 billion.

These people will have to be fed. For now, there is so much food in some parts of the world that books about diets lead the best-seller lists. Obesity and the health problems that arise from overeating exist in the same world where people are starving to death. There is land with the potential to produce more food and vast ocean resources, but neither are infinite and certainly will not be adequate if we continue to upset the natural balance by polluting our environment with industrial toxic wastes, or destroying habitats by over-building, or depleting our supply of food by overfarming or overfishing.

Food from the seas and oceans is the world's hope as populations increase. Carelessness and deliberate abuse have caused widespread pollution of these most valuable present and future food resources. In many places in the world fish are contaminated with heavy metals and their use as food banned.

We waste a great deal of food. Here in New York's Fulton Fish Market, fish that are not sold rot; unpopular species of fish caught in nets and trawls are often just discarded, feeding no one, disrupting the natural balance in the oceans.

We will see well-meaning responses to hunger around the world. We will see how many well-intentioned plans have gone awry, causing the problem to worsen. We will witness human greed and see how corruption has kept the poor from receiving aid that could have saved them.

Frances Moore Lappé, an expert on international problems associated with hunger and foreign aid, wrote, "Field investigations and other research have led us to realize that U.S. foreign assistance fails to help the poor because it is of necessity based on one fundamental fallacy: That aid can reach the powerless even though channeled through the powerful."

In a letter to the World Neighbors Program, workers who were involved in free food distribution to victims of an earthquake in Guatemala wrote something of a universal truth when they said: "Food being brought into an area inevitably reduces the demand for locally produced food. This is especially true when large quantities are involved. . . . This distribution of imported food lowers prices of locally produced food. . . . This may take away from the people their previous ability to provide for themselves and create a new, unnecessary dependency."

We have introduced the problems of poverty and plenty, of limited food resources, of failure of human moral responsibility, and have raised the issue of keeping the fragile balance of local economies and indigenous food-growing and distribution systems intact in the developing world, even when we help relieve starvation. We will look at these issues in greater detail, along with some ugly aspects of the politics of hunger, which, as we will see, rear up in the real world of foreign assistance.

I often speak about matters relating to hunger and the environment to groups of young people concerned about the problems and contemporary issues of our times. The idealism young people bring to the analysis of world hunger is what prompted me to write this book. Young people see things with the simplicity of truth: Something is right or it is wrong. If a little child is hungry, that child must be fed. There is the simple truth about what must be done. There are no adult hang-ups, no rationalizations for not helping.

The most frequent question young people pose after learning about hunger is: What can I do to help?

There is a lot anyone willing to help can do. As you will see, hunger and human need may exist right around the corner from where you live. A person does not always have to look off into the far corners of the world to find people in need. People who are homeless, without proper food or clothing, can often be found close to home.

There are many organizations established to help. Some of these are listed at the end of this book. On Halloween, young people obtain from their schools little donation boxes for contributions to UNICEF. If enough young people picked up discarded soda cans and deposit bottles and kept the refunds in a special place until the UNICEF box was passed around at school, imagine the impact

Homeless persons gathered this bread from garbage leavings outside a food store and brought it to their cardboard shanty shelter at the exit of the United Nations garage. Perhaps this symbol, outside the world body charged with the care and keeping of humanity, describes a human condition: Hunger in the midst of plenty.

nationwide. From litter, thousands of hungry children could be fed.

Finding projects that can be acted on by scouts, at school, through clubs and houses of worship will not only help others, but will pay dividends in personal satisfaction and education. Time and energy may be put into helping prepare meals for a local soup kitchen, as the young people described later in this book have done, or sponsoring a foster child in a foreign country, or raising money for a worthwhile fund to help the needy.

Most important of all is to learn about the problems of hunger. Read, study, go to the library and ask the reference librarian to help you find materials about aspects of the problem that interest you most. But even before you go further in this book, stop. Stop here. Look at the clock and time one minute. When that minute is gone, you will know one thing with certainty: that in this world, your world, twenty-four people have starved to death.

If you have a little brother or sister or friend, pick him or her up; judge the child's weight; then ask yourself: How far could I carry that child? A block? From your town to another city? A hundred miles? Ask yourself whether you could carry your brother or sister or little friend that far if neither of you had any food to eat. Then you will understand the agony of people pictured in this book, carrying little children along the Hunger Road, hoping to find help, knowing that if they do not find it their children will die.

Some people may expect to find easy solutions here. There are none. Travel now where I have traveled, see with my eyes some of what I have seen, then use your own eyes to identify problems and people in need and follow the dictates of your heart to help them. For you see, after all that can be said is said, love is the only real solution.

1
CAMBODIA:
The Anthropology of Crisis

They are everywhere, huge craters resembling water holes.
At first I thought they were water holes, so round, so sym-
metrical and filled with water. It's an impression that didn't
last very long.

NOTEBOOK ENTRY MADE FLYING OVER
CAMBODIA, FEBRUARY 3, 1975.

The United States Air Force called it "Operation Menu." But what
was served during a fourteen-month period in 1969 and 1970 were
bombs, not food: 108,823 tons of bombs in B-52 raids over Cambodia. It was surely these air raids over Cambodian territory and the
subsequent American ground action that brought that part of the
war to the attention of the world; Cambodia, previously, was only
a launching pad for guerrilla attacks upon American forces in Vietnam.

No exact statistics are available of the total tonnages used by U.S.
aircraft in tactical strikes over Cambodian soil, but for an eight-
month period beginning in July 1970, Defense Department records
show that some eight thousand sorties were flown. The Pentagon
reported that air and ground munitions used in all of Southeast Asia
(Cambodia, Vietnam, and Laos) between 1966 and August 17,
1973, totaled 15,228,324 tons. Of this, 7,494,806 tons of bombs
were dropped by air. Compare this with the 2,057,244 tons of bombs
dropped by U.S. forces in every theater of operation during World
War II and the approximately 635,000 tons of bombs dropped by
the U.S. forces during the Korean War.

Bomb craters were everywhere; devastation was everywhere. What the bombing hadn't destroyed, five years of savage ground fighting and rocket attacks had, in a nation with a population in mid-1973 of about 7.8 million people living in an area of 70,000 square miles, approximately the size of Oklahoma.

These war statistics were reduced to understandable human terms by the outwardly tough medical director of the World Vision Relief Organization, Dr. Penelope Key. On the verge of tears when she returned from conducting a clinic for Cambodian refugees, Dr. Key said, "I've had a perfectly dreadful morning. The children are dying all over the place." And they were. Not only from the traumatic wounds of warfare, but from malnutrition. In February 1975, children were starving to death.

The plight of the Cambodians in those last weeks of the war didn't start there. Some say it began in 1970. Others insist that a fuller historical analysis is necessary to properly understand the Cambodian crisis.

CAMBODIA IN PERSPECTIVE

A vassal state in the first century A.D., Cambodia was part of the Chinese Funan empire. The people were called Khmers. Slowly the Khmer tribes drifted southward. In the sixth century, they overthrew Funan domination. Bloody civil war broke out and continued until 802. The accession of King Jayavarman II brought peace and with it the golden age of Khmer peoples. The ruins of Angkor, Jayavarman II's imperial city, remain as mute testimony to the might and majesty of the early Cambodian empire. Khmers then ruled over what is now Thailand, Laos, South Vietnam, and Cambodia. A series of wars with the Chams, Thai, and Vietnamese ate away at Cambodia's power until, by the beginning of the nineteenth century, Cambodia was reduced to its present borders.

At Cambodian King Ang Duong's request, France established a protectorate over Cambodia in 1863. Nineteen-year-old King Norodom Sihanouk had ascended to the Cambodian throne in 1941, elected by a Crown Council. He began a campaign against French

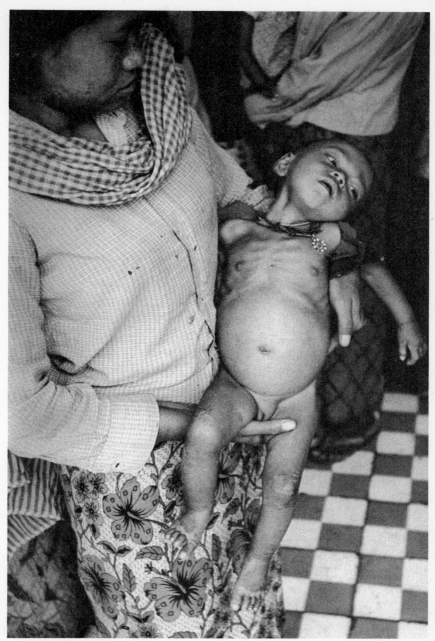

Little children, their bodies swollen, stomachs distended, skin peeling off from the effects of kwashiorkor, the lack of protein in their diets, starved to death.

rule in 1952, going into voluntary exile in June 1953. Sihanouk refused to return to Phnom Penh until Cambodia was independent from France. Throughout this period, savage fighting between French and Viet Minh forces (a coalition of anti-French Vietnamese groups) raged in Vietnam. Then, on May 7, 1954, the Vietnamese city of Dien Bien Phu fell and France surrendered. The next day a peace conference was held in Geneva. Cambodia, Laos, the state of Vietnam, the Democratic Republic of Vietnam (represented by the Viet Minh), France, China, Russia, and Great Britain participated. The results included negotiated cease-fire agreements known as the Geneva Agreements of 1954.

THE RECENT PAST

Cambodia, emerging from the devastation in Indochina into the political unrest of the late fifties, declared neutrality. Communist attacks in Laos and Vietnam continued. North Vietnamese army troops entered and controlled whole provinces in Cambodia by mid-1960. On March 29, 1970, the communists put into action a strategy designed to establish complete territorial control of the 600-mile Cambodia–South Vietnam coastline.

President Nixon on April 30, 1970, announced that the United States and South Vietnam would launch a two-month military operation against communist-controlled territory in Cambodia. The Cambodian government approved. Although cross-border operations ended on June 30, 1970, the Cambodian military, supported by arms and material from the U.S. Military Assistance Program, continued fighting, but they lost ground as the war grew more intense. Finally, by 1975 the Cambodian government controlled only enclaves in the major population centers. These enclaves were surrounded by the enemy and cut off from one another except by air.

Unable to plant or fish except in secure zones within government-controlled areas, Cambodians living within the enclaves were forced to rely on airlifted rice. Refugees from the countryside continually pressed into the city of Phnom Penh and the other enclaves. They

Memories of the upheaval and flight from home will probably mark these Cambodian youngsters forever. *(UNICEF photo by Jacques Danois)*

had been driven from their homes in the countryside by the fighting, guerrilla raids, fear, and a deliberate policy of terror. The steady stream of refugees strained the already overburdened urban centers. An estimated two million refugees crowded into Phnom Penh, which had a 375,000 prewar population.

These gentle people were shocked and stunned by the terrorists' violence. Typical was the raid on Kompong Speu, a refugee camp established by Catholic Relief Services. The entire village was burned to the ground; twenty women and children were killed, their bodies cut open, mutilated. Ten children were kidnapped by the raiders. Later they, too, were found dead along the roadside, their throats cut.

The horror of this incident is that it was not one isolated act committed by war-crazed guerrillas, but part of a deliberate policy of premeditated cruelty. Cruelty heaped upon devastation, bombing, and warfare.

This was a Catholic Relief Services refugee camp. The ashes mark small huts where families were sheltered. Pol Pot's Khmer Rouge forces attacked this camp and threw grenades into the huts, killing the refugees who had barely survived the war. Children kidnapped from this camp were later found along the roadside with their throats cut. The ravages of war bring death quickly and cruelly; war also results in the disruption of life, so that the people in developing countries cannot plant or fish, and death results just as surely in the end.

THE HUMAN CONDITION

The food situation in Cambodia in early 1975 was one of impending disaster. Government troops traditionally went to the front with their wives and children. Battle casualties took a higher toll of the families than the soldiers, but, without their wives to care for them, the soldiers could not eat. There was no system of commissary or mess. Soldiers, when they were paid, were paid at the front. There was no means for them to get the money to their families, if they weren't with them. Leaving a family behind meant that soldiers' children would starve.

Tarps and tents serve as refugee shelter. Hundreds of thousands of people were
displaced by the fighting in Cambodia. They often fled to the cities, living without
means of support, without food or shelter. International relief organizations tried to
respond to the crisis by supplying tarps to shield these people from the elements.

Moving from battlefront to battlefront, wives could not plant their gardens. They had to rely on what they could buy. Food was sold at inflated prices. The poor could not buy enough for their families.

The bulk of refugees entering Phnom Penh and other provincial capitals were farmers from neighboring countrysides. The impact of this influx of farmers into urban areas away from productive farmlands reduced agricultural production to the point where Cambodia, once an exporter of rice, fruit, fish, and livestock, had to depend on massive imports.

Incidence of vitamin B deficiency and beri beri among the city's poor and military men gave sad testimony to the fact that the people could no longer supplement their diets with fruit or fish.

Measurements of weight, height, and upper arm circumference give good indications of child nutrition. A healthy two-year-old child by International Standards should weigh 12.4 kilograms. A sampling of Cambodian two year olds weighed in January 1975 averaged 7.85 kilograms.

Arm circumference for Cambodian two year olds measured 11.96 centimeters in January 1975. The norm for healthy children of this age is 16.3 centimeters.

No child in the sample tested reached the International Standards of weight for age or arm circumference for age. These tests confirmed the universal opinion of those involved in Cambodian health and nutrition relief efforts that children were starving to death.

Malnutrition, including advanced stages of kwashiorkor (a protein deficiency disease) and marasmus (severe wasting away of a child's body in advanced stages of hunger) were rampant. The state of children's health was such that ordinary, simple childhood maladies were often fatal. Children were dying of complications brought on by enteritis (inflammation of the intestines), flu, measles, and respiratory diseases. Their resistance to all disease was low, and the terrible conditions under which they were forced to live caused epidemics.

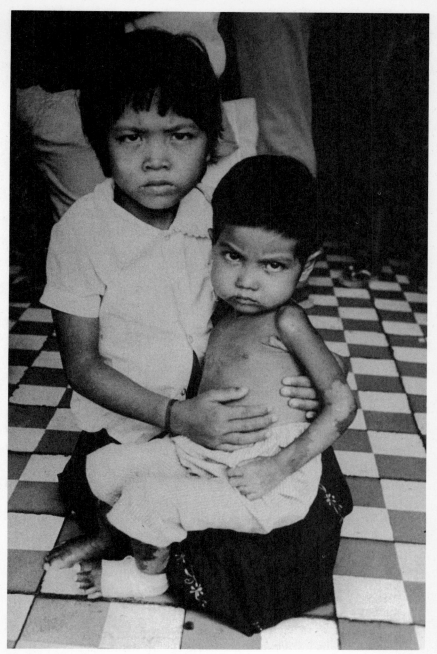

Her little brother is gravely ill with kwashiorkor.

Doctors from the International Red Cross reported that "Malnutrition now exists on a large scale . . . complications are stronger now in malnourished children . . . it is getting worse—in our refugee camps it is getting worse. Thousands and thousands of children may be tipping over. Kawshiorkor, . . . usually a disease in age 2 to 4 years, is occurring in 10 year olds. There is no hope for the future. Tuberculosis is increasing. Cholera and typhoid have started in January (1975)."

Dr. Dean Kroh, medical director of the Christian Missionary Alliance, reported: "As time went on we realized we could not cope with the numerous cases of malnutrition that came for care. . . . We have seen in the last six months among the poor of the cities who are not receiving regular food supplements considerable increase in both number and severity of cases of malnutrition in the children under five years of age. There is also an increase in older children with malnutrition, up to fourteen years of age; in pregnant women and mothers who have just given birth; and in people over fifty years of age. Each clinic session will include up to five older people suffering from moderate to severe forms of vitamin B deficiencies with varying degrees of heart failure. We were not seeing this many older people so affected, even a year ago. Another gauge of malnutrition can be the degree of anemia. The average hemoglobin we find in children is 6 to 7 grams. This about half of what it should be. The main cause is low protein intake, plus other diseases such as hookworm, malaria, and tuberculosis among the children. Poor nutrition plays a definite part in the diseases' appearance."

Monthly statistics from the Tuol Kuak nutrition center for December 1974 and January 1975 document the condition of the children who were admitted. The director reported, "It seems impossible to think that the children can arrive at this center any sicker than now or that families can be in any more desperate circumstances."

Hospitals were overcrowded beyond belief. Patients on stretchers filled the halls until the stretchers were needed, and then patients

Families would come, would walk for many miles, hoping for help, flocking to the already overcrowded relief hospitals and clinics. Many had to be turned away, most certainly to die.

were put on the floor. Dispensaries, clinics, hospitals, and nutrition centers, limited in number, were forced to refuse treatment to the gravely ill because of the lack of facilities and shortage of doctors. Overworked medical personnel were unable to cope with the numbers of people who presented themselves for treatment. The facilities were not only overcrowded but, for the most part, they were also crude and unsanitary. There was an acute shortage of medicines and drugs. Death frequently resulted from infection and lack of proper care; medication often was not administered to patients suffering severed limbs or gross traumatic abdominal wounds.

In clinics doctors walked among the sick with a marking pen. They numbered childrens' arms, sorting the sick from the most sick. In numbering patients up to the maximum they could see, some doctors gave children priority. One doctor said, "All those people are sick. Seventy-five percent are children. We saw only the worst cases. Fifty children should have been admitted this morning. I took only six kids. We only had six beds." Thousands were being turned away.

It requires little imagination to picture these wretchedly frail and sickly little bodies, borne away in their weak mothers' arms, carried to a shanty hovel, a concrete stadium bench, or a dirty alley somewhere, to die; certain to suffer, then to die, untreated, unhospitalized, unfed.

The overall medical picture during this period is indicated by the fact that most hospitals provided no food to patients. They had to depend on their families not only to obtain food but to prepare it. Major surgery was performed in crude circumstances, often without sufficient drugs and without whole blood or serums. Patients with traumatic blast injuries suffered because of inadequate supplies of painkilling drugs. Operating rooms were crudely furnished, unclean, and without many sterile precautions. In provincial hospitals, operating rooms often consisted of a single room in a dilapidated building furnished with a bloodstained wooden table and a few surgical instruments. Bloody remnants of previous surgical cases were left on the floor.

An older brother holding this dying child. The sadness and grief in his face tell the bitter story of Cambodia's tragedy.

These conditions existed in a country where the doctor-to-patient ratio was 1 to 16,710 people, compared to a 1 to 600 ratio in the United States, and where civilian and military war casualties took a large proportion of doctors' time. Between the first and twentieth of February 1975, military casualties amounted to 11,812. Of these 1,857 were deaths. Not surprisingly, in one hospital 30 percent of the seriously wounded died.

In the overcrowded hospitals, unattended wounds were exposed to the dirt and filth; the stink of pus and infection mingled with the foul odor from clogged and flooded toilets. Critically wounded waited long hours for any treatment; there were not enough doctors to go around. In these traumatic circumstances, it is obvious that children suffering from malnutrition could not find treatment or care.

Then Cambodia fell. Brutally, violently, suddenly. Forces under Pol Pot, leader of the insurgent Khmer Rouge, occupied Phnom Penh on April 17, 1975, and a systematic program of genocide was implemented by the communist regime. Hospitals were emptied of sick and wounded. People were driven out of the cities and towns. Physicians, nurses, anyone connected with the former regime, educated people and intellectuals, even those who wore eyeglasses, were clubbed to death, shot, or stoned. Millions were killed or died of starvation. Fields ran red with blood, killing fields.

Sydney Schanberg, a reporter for the *New York Times* working in Cambodia, and his assistant Dith Pran remained behind. Schanberg managed to reach an embassy compound and get out of the country, but Pran was a Cambodian. He was trapped in a nightmare of death and violence that was the subject of a book and film about Cambodia. Pran survived by hiding his identity, pretending to be a simple peasant. He survived a nonlife, witness to the sort of holocaust the world has not seen since the revelation of Nazi extermination camps at the close of World War II.

"When you didn't starve it feel sour, but when you are starving it is very sweet," Pran said, describing eating leaves to survive. "I saw

A refugee child who, with the help of relief agencies and foreign donors, has been able to stave off the effects of starvation. He has planted a small "garden" and is justly proud of his accomplishment. Shortly after this picture was taken the Communist forces under Pol Pot invaded and drove the refugees into the country, killing many thousands along the way.

many killing fields everywhere. They kill people like you kill the fly or mosquito," Pran continued, recounting the horror after the Americans pulled out and seven days later Phnom Penh fell.

"I didn't want to believe they were killing people, but they did it. You don't want to believe the unthinkable," Sydney Schanberg said, describing brutality inconceivable in human terms. "Holocaust. You can use that word. A civilization has been erased," Schanberg told me.

Monsignor Robert Charlebois, former Catholic Relief Services director for Southeast Asia and the Pacific, witnessed the tragic results as starving refugees escaped Cambodia and flocked to refugee camps in neighboring Thailand. Monsignor Charlebois had served five years as CRS program director in Vietnam. "They are driving the refugees in front of them like cattle. The refugees are their shield and the Khmer Rouge hide among them," Monsignor Bob said, describing the plight of the escapees who managed to make it to the Thai border often only to be machine-gunned or forced to turn back. Hardened border patrols were under pressure to discourage the massive outpouring of refugees.

Vietnamese regular troops invaded Cambodia in December 1978, forcing Pol Pot's troops out of Phnom Penh and into the mountains, where guerrilla warfare continues. In all of this the refugees are used as pawns.

The Vietnamese occupying forces, who continue to battle with remnants of Pol Pot's cadre of Khmer Rouge, opened mass graves whose piles of cadavers and skeletons were put on display for visiting members of the international press. This is a chronicle of current events. How history will finally tally the events in Cambodia in human terms is still unknown. In fact, the toll of those who died and are dying in Cambodia may never be fully known.

Malnutrition does not take place overnight; starvation is a slow and painful process and its victims usually succumb to disease before they die from lack of food. If there could be a glimmer of hope for these people in peril, then it is that the soil is fertile in Cambodia,

A family awaits aid at a refugee camp.

the rivers rich with fish. If they can plant the fields, if they have seeds, if they can fish, then perhaps they will survive—some of them. Even so, Cambodia shall continue to be a wound on civilization, and the scar may remain forever.

2

ETHIOPIA:
Hidden Treachery While Death
Stalks the Poor

There is a reckless disregard for the sensibilities of people that so often appears in books about American officials overseas. The talking through people, as though their presence doesn't exist. They don't see the children dying; they don't look.

NOTEBOOK ENTRY MADE WHILE DRIVING ALONG A
MUDDY ROAD IN ETHIOPIA, AUGUST 1974.

Ethiopia is strategically located on the Red Sea between the Sudan to the north and west, Somalia and Kenya to the south. Across the narrow stretch of water to the east are Yemen and Saudi Arabia. Nestled on a corner of Ethiopia's coastline sits the former French Territory of Afars and Issas known as Djibouti. Ethiopia's position at the narrow entrance to the Red Sea gives the nation control over access to the Suez Canal and thus control over sea traffic, including oil shipments, from the gulf states.

Ethiopia's geography underscores the country's importance to the United States and other military powers. Comprising an area of 472,000 square miles, about the size of Texas, Oklahoma, and New Mexico combined, with a population of some 44 million, Ethiopia is a tribal nation where a primitive feudal system virtually enslaves the people. It is Africa's oldest independent country. Legend has it that Menelik I, the son of King Solomon and the queen

A mother in Ethiopia awaits grain distribution.

of Sheba, began the empire of Ethiopia, and the monarchy he founded has continued to modern times. In 1930 Haile Selassie was crowned emperor of Ethiopia. The country was occupied by Italy in 1936, but Selassie was returned to power at the end of World War II.

After the war, the United States maintained military installations in Ethiopia and an active military assistance program. U.S. intelligence activities were conducted in Ethiopia's northern province of Eritrea at an American base called Kagnew Station. While aware of Emperor Haile Selassie's dictatorial cruelty and the corruption of his government, the United States considered him a stabilizing force in Africa. But Selassie was toppled on September 12, 1974, in the midst of a famine where hundreds of thousands of Ethiopians had starved to death in a country where those in power stole or wasted food sent to feed the hungry and sold for profit Ethiopian-grown food grains that could have been used to save the starving.

The totalitarian regime of Haile Selassie was replaced in 1974 by a totalitarian Armed Forces Committee. This ruthless Marxist government conducted purges. In a five-month period in 1977 and 1978 known as the "Red Terror" more than ten thousand people opposed to the regime were murdered.

Ethiopia has been at war since the monarchy's ouster. In the northern province of Eritrea, a violent rebellion and guerrilla warfare are claiming a large toll of casualties. In the southern Ogaden region, an invasion by neighboring Somalia, which lays claim to the ethnic Somali area of Ethiopia, was repulsed; however, terrorist and guerrilla attacks continue, as does the brutal fighting.

What went on in Ethiopia, what is going on in Ethiopia, is a tragic story of corruption and deceit, where the exploitation of famine is big business. Innocent people starved because they were deliberately starved, because of incompetence and poor planning, or because of neglect.

We will explore Ethiopia's deliberate use of starvation as a political tool and of helter-skelter relief efforts as political ploys used to manipulate world public opinion and foreign aid.

DROUGHT AND FAMINE

There have always been periods of drought in sub-Saharan Africa. Yet in this sparse and desolate area, tribes of nomadic peoples have survived for centuries. There had been six years of high rainfall in the region beginning in 1961, which encouraged increased settlement and larger cattle herds grazing on the renewed scraggly desert pasturelands. The United States Agency for International Development (AID) came to the area to help, building 1,400 wells, encouraging further settlement and increased herds. All of this was done without regard to the fragile nature of the desert environment and the centuries of natural balance, which kept herds and population density low so that the land could support them.

The high rainfall slowed again, bringing drought to the region in 1968. To support the herds, trees were cut down so the animals could eat the leaves. Even the roots of trees were eaten by foraging herds. This assured eventual disaster, but rains came again in 1969, postponing the inevitable. Then, as had happened in the region over history, rainfall diminished, and three years of drought followed. By 1973, many herds of cattle had died and the increased population, which had been encouraged by the wells and AID projects to settle in the region, suffered. The onslaught of disaster in the desert had begun. The problem would be covered up officially, perhaps to prevent accusations of blame for bad judgment, but whatever the reason, delays in reporting the disaster caused thousands of people to suffer and die of starvation.

This drought passed eventually, and in time life returned to the region. A decade later, tragedy and drought struck again. For Ethiopia, the only thing that had changed was the government; for the people in the affected regions, death and disaster returned unchecked.

THE COVER-UP

In 1974, after a long delay, the public was finally made aware that 100,000 persons, by conservative estimates (other reliable reports indicated as many as 500,000), had starved to death in Ethiopia. It

Top: In Ethiopia most of the population rely on traditional farming with simple tools to subsist. When the drought came and their crops failed, their animals died, their way of life ended, and they became refugees.

Bottom: Water is a precious commodity. It is never wasted, and often people have to dig to find it and have to carry it many miles.

was only then that an international cover-up of the Ethiopian drought during the last seven months of 1973 came to light.

A special report issued by the Carnegie Endowment for International Peace put it plainly: "The embassies of the United States (which included more than twenty-five U.S. AID workers in Addis Ababa alone), West Germany, Sweden, Britain, France, the leaders of the OAU (Organization of African Unity) and three UN (United Nations) specialized agencies—WHO (World Health Organization), FAO (Food and Agriculture Organization), and UNICEF (The UN Children's Fund)—all participated along with the UN Development Programme in the cover-up."

The Carnegie report added: "Officials from these countries and organizations knew about the disaster but chose to remain silent rather than jeopardize working relationships with Ethiopian officials." This inaction in the face of disaster created unnecessary delay in staving off the horror of starvation and resulted in havoc when relief efforts were finally begun.

DISASTER IS GOOD BUSINESS

At the height of the 1974 famine, I was sent from Washington as a diplomatic official attached to the State Department's Inspectorate General to investigate conditions in Ethiopia and report on the relief efforts. I was immediately confronted with the fact that there was then and had always been a supply of food grains in Ethiopia, which could have stemmed the famine and fed the poor. These food stocks were being sold, allowed to spoil, and otherwise manipulated while children starved.

A church worker in Addis Ababa, the Ethiopian capital, told me that he was continually confronted with offers by grain merchants to sell him locally grown corn. The price he had been quoted— $9.50 per 220 pounds plus $3.00 for shipping it to the drought-stricken provinces—was very reasonable compared to the high cost of shipping in relief supplies. The offer this relief worker received was for as much as 220,000 pounds of corn. When I inquired

There were always enough food grains and transportation available in Ethiopia to feed the starving.

whether these offers were easily available, the church worker told me, "I could find them every day. One man promised delivery of five hundred fifty thousand pounds per day. This is true today, and it has always been true."

When I asked about transportation for the food so that it could reach the needy, the church representative affirmed, "There is not one day since February that I could not get four hundred trucks. But no one would pay for them. This government is not human at all." I took samples of the grain the church worker had received and placed them in sealed evidence bags.

In order to verify the church worker's information, I posed as a grain buyer, and went into the grain markets of Addis Ababa. Grain was piled up in huge quantities, with trucks standing by ready to transport it. I went about taking pictures, obtaining price quotations, and taking samples of the grains offered for sale. The price I was generally quoted was $9.25 per 220 pounds. When I asked one merchant his name, he refused, saying, "You can understand because of these times."

I took my samples to the U.S. Embassy in Addis Ababa and showed them to an American grain expert without telling him where I obtained them. The expert studied the kernels carefully. He identified one group as U.S.-grown flint corn. "Perfectly good for eating," he said. Of another sample, the expert said, "Looks like it was grown here." He admired the quality of the samples I produced saying, "In Africa you hardly see anything this good."

Samples of corn and wheat obtained by the author with the prices and quantities that were available on the open market in Ethiopia at a time when people were starving to death. The author posed in an undercover capacity to obtain the evidence while investigating the diversion of relief grains for the U.S. State Department. Grain experts identified some of the corn as coming from the U.S., obviously stolen from relief shipments and being sold in the commercial markets. Prices quoted are in Ethiopian currency; one U.S. dollar equals two Ethiopian dollars.

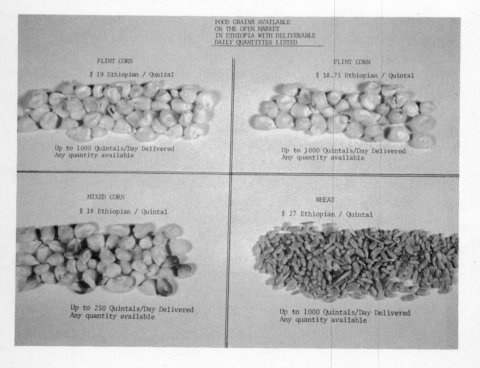

FOOD GRAINS AVAILABLE ON THE OPEN MARKET IN ETHIOPIA WITH DELIVERABLE DAILY QUANTITIES LISTED

FLINT CORN
$ 19 Ethiopian / Qunital
Up to 1000 Quintals/Day Delivered
Any quantity available

FLINT CORN
$ 18.75 Ethiopian / Quintal
Up to 1000 Quintals/Day Delivered
Any quantity available

MIXED CORN
$ 18 Ethiopian / Quintal
Up to 250 Quintals/Day Delivered
Any quantity available

WHEAT
$ 27 Ethiopian / Quintal
Up to 1000 Quintals/Day Delivered
Any quantity available

All of the grain samples I obtained were of good, edible quality. I returned to the grain markets and recorded more data on grain samples. I verified that many heavy-duty trucks were being loaded with grains and was told that one year earlier grain had also been available in quantity in the same market. All during the famine, food had always been available in Ethiopia! People from the drought-afflicted regions of Ethiopia were starving because they were being starved.

From July 1973 to June 1974, the United States and other donor countries spent 25 million dollars to supply free food grains to Ethiopia. As of June 15, 1974, U.S. AID had contributed 64,418 metric tons of wheat, sorghum, corn, and instant corn-soya milk, valued at over fifteen-and-a-half million dollars, for famine relief. Other international donors pledged over 80,000 metric tons of grain. Nonfood assistance from the United States totaled more than 2 million dollars. In sum, as of mid-1974, the United States contributed nearly 18 million dollars for relief.

During this same period, the Ethiopian government spent nothing for grain for the needy. In fact, the 1973 harvest in Ethiopia resulted in an estimated surplus of about 45,000 metric tons of food grains, which were expected to be left unsold when the 1974 harvest arrived. Ethiopian grain exports in 1973 of about 9,000 metric tons were almost double the previous year's exports. During the height of the 1974 Ethiopian famine, cereal export totals were 7,941 metric tons. Yet for want of a little food, children died by the thousands.

With the $9.25 per 220 pounds price in hand, I asked a U.S. AID official what it cost to deliver relief food grain to Ethiopia. "Was it one thousand dollars per ton?" I asked this U.S. official.

"That sounds pretty close," he replied.

"Could it have been as much as fifteen hundred dollars per ton?" I asked. This high-ranking U.S. Embassy official wasn't sure, but what was certain was that it cost a lot more than $92.50 plus $30 delivery per ton, the amount I could have bought it for in the Addis markets.

Disaster was good business for the Ethiopian government. While children were starving to death, Ethiopian government officials exported food for profit—including U.S. disaster-relief food. The Ethiopian government flourished economically. In 1973, when thousands of Ethiopians were dying, the foreign exchange reserves of Ethiopia increased from 100 million dollars to 200 million dollars. This is hard foreign currency. During the first five months of 1974, when Ethiopia was appealing for large-scale emergency relief and rehabilitation assistance from the world, its foreign-exchange reserves increased another 100 million dollars. The Ethiopian government, with 300 million dollars in hard foreign exchange, had sufficient resources to buy its grain requirements. Once the truth about the disaster was publicized in the media, U.S. and international donors spent in the course of one year 25 million dollars supplying free food grains to Ethiopia. Ethiopia in this time spent nothing for grain for its needy, despite the assurances of the Ethiopian government that it would do so.

At a time when the United States and other donor nations were being called upon to supply, in an emergency airlift, such things as tires, tubes, and other commodities, my inquiries at local stores revealed that ample supplies of these items were also available on the market. There was never any need to specially airlift these goods into the country.

Ethiopian leaders hoarded large herds of cattle that they had bought up from peasants during the drought. It was reported that one tribal chief had a herd of some 70,000 cattle, in this country whose herds were allegedly decimated by the drought.

MURDER

Al Temple, a veteran U.S. AID pilot who had flown throughout Ethiopia observing waste, theft, mismanagement, and deliberate cover-ups, emphasized what many had said: The drought was being used by the Imperial Ethiopian Government to murder political foes.

"The civilian authorities and army personnel are discriminating in grain distribution. People in the Ogaden area are members of

The rains finally came, but too late to save many of the herds. Often the animals had to be sold at distressed prices to wealthy chiefs who had purposely withheld relief grains until they made great fortunes from the misery of the poor.

nomadic Somali tribes. Ethiopians don't consider them Ethiopian, so they don't care if they die," Al Temple explained.

"The government officials don't care if the nomads live or die. Two years ago, in 1972, I showed Ethiopian government officials dead cattle. They paid no attention. It was only when the drought moved in from the lowlands to the highlands and began affecting their own people (the ruling class's tribe), it was only then that the relief effort started at all," Al Temple told me.

Al Temple's report was substantiated by Ted Ford, a career diplomat attached to the Political Section of the U.S. Embassy in Addis Ababa. Ford stated bluntly: "The Ethiopian government is not sending grain out since the people who would receive it are the political outs. The government of Ethiopia is purposely starving them."

Ford continued: "The U.S. AID program is being badly used. . . . Corrupt Ethiopian government officials are being protected by AID."

The irony, according to Paul Russel, Director of America's Food for Peace Program, was that Ethiopian merchants were exporting food grains for profit to Somalia.

Again and again, American officials shook their heads in dismay over the politics of starvation and the treachery of the Ethiopian ruling class. The U.S. State Department's acting Washington desk officer for Ethiopia said: "The central government did not want to pay any attention to what was happening in Ethiopia. In the north, the people living there never cared much for Haile Selassie, and the reaction of the central government was reciprocated toward these people in terms of not providing them with any drought relief."

Officials at the World Bank echoed awareness of discrimination in relief distribution. The directors of the East Africa Division of the World Bank and the Bank's Ethiopia program officer and staff economist for Ethiopia, related similar abuses. "We know that the farmers were forced to sell their land, but we don't know to whom," a World Bank official told me.

All during this time, Steve O'Brien, the World Bank's staff economist for Ethiopia, related the true condition: "The Ethiopian Government Grain Corporation could have been used last year if the government was responsive. Grain was available in the Corporation and it could have been moved with timely government intervention. It was just that the government did not care about the problem last year."

The U.S. AID mission director in Ethiopia, Dr. John L. Withers, responding to these charges in August 1974, said, "I tried to do all that was possible to urge the Ethiopian government to buy surplus grain. . . . There was a lackadaisical attitude on the part of the Ethiopian government."

FOOD ROTTING IN THE PORTS

I inspected Ethiopian port storage areas and was shown some 830 tons of sweetened powdered milk that had arrived ten days before. Much of the cargo was damaged or destroyed. The company representative said about 400 tons, or half the powdered milk, had suffered water damage in shipping. Relief supplies from France were also heavily damaged. Of 325 tons of butter oil from France, 20 tons were damaged, and many of the containers were leaking. I was told they had been damaged in the unloading. The sweetened powdered milk, packaged in paper bags, was stored outside without any covering or protection.

The Ethiopian director of transport told me that the food here as well as the food stored at the end of the airport and at the town of Serdo was spoiled. It was not fit for human consumption. A nightmare, in a nation where people were starving.

Tons of food arrived. U.S. AID officials did not meet the ships when they docked nor did they inspect the food shipments. Grain that had come so far and cost the American people so much was contaminated with oil and seawater, and much of what wasn't spoiled on board the ships rotted on the docks. Tons of corn lay there, the U.S. AID bags burst open by long exposure, their spilled contents rotting in the African sun.

Foodstuffs for relief were not the only commodities at the ports.

U.S. AID relief supplies left to rot in the Ethiopian ports (top), and in storage (bottom), wasted while children died of starvation for want of a little food.

Two new American military helicopters sat among some thirty new Fiat trucks, trucks that were going nowhere. The trucks were shipped in at great expense to haul relief grain.

One port official provided me with photographs he had taken of U.S. grain that had been in port more than half a year. "The bags broke open," he said, then recounted the spoilage and the extra expense for new bags and rebagging.

The official documented this case history: "The corn was stored in the open. No tarps were put over it. The bags were plastic, so there was no aeration. The corn was first stored in a warehouse. Then it was moved outside. It cost five hundred Djibouti francs per one hundred kilograms to move the grain. The grain bags tore open because of the heat. It had to be rebagged at one hundred seventy to one hundred eighty Djibouti francs for the bags and the labor had to be paid."

Freight forwarders denounced the corruption of Ethiopian officials. Several Djibouti forwarders shrugged, suggesting fraud was something everyone expected. A fact of life.

RELIEF GRAIN ROTTING IN THE PROVINCES

After reports of the scandal began to appear, bottlenecks at the ports were broken and grain was dumped in massive quantities in the provinces. Officials in the field complained. They were overwhelmed. The man responsible for grain distribution in Wollo Province said: "Now the problem is, we have too much grain going in there. . . . You will see tons piled up. Everything came in massive quantities. In the interior they gave the food grains to anyone who wanted it. . . . They started at a massive level without accounting for it. They got two months supply all at once; it would be better if they stored the grain at the ports. There are no selective surveys to tell which people are the needy and which not needy. People who don't need it are getting it. There's fifty thousand quintals [a quintal is 220 pounds] in the Kombolcha Airport hangar. We have thirty-five hundred metric tons of wheat and corn, only half of which has been distributed. The governors keep saying they need it. Bankers and store owners are all getting grain. The real drought belt between the highlands and desert is only getting a trickle. People are becoming militant. They think it's their right; they are not deserving of grain. There is no starvation here."

This report came from an American. It was substantiated by an Ethiopian. The American at the distribution site shook his head in dismay, commenting: "Grain in local markets is worthless. There is so much of it. Here we had a food-for-work program. The workers were given, in return for work, a three-week supply of grain. They don't want it. I was here one year ago. I saw an adequate supply of grain in this town."

The same theme was echoed throughout Ethiopia. A Frenchman operating an orphan shelter whispered to me in French: "There was ample grain. It was being stolen."

In other areas, places where there were needy persons, areas where disfavored tribes lived, I observed men, women, and children waiting for food. In one place I was told by refugees that they had been waiting for five days outside an Ethiopian warehouse. At another place, hundreds of refugees surrounded our Jeep. They had been waiting nine days and no one knew whether there would be anything for them. At one location, people were waiting in the cold for grain. They had been waiting ten days.

Farmers who lost their crops in another area came two days' walk and slept in the streets to get food. They told me the landlords for whom they were tenant farmers refused to give them grain. They had no seeds to plant. The Ethiopian official with the key to the food storehouse was nowhere to be found. Fifty thousand quintals of grain were stored there. An Ethiopian with me who worked at the U.S. Embassy related how he had been at this location before, and the man with the key to the storehouse could not be found at that time either. In that province, we went to the governor's office. The governor decided he would himself inspect the grain in storage. He admitted he had received reports that there was a lot of spoilage. He said this was due to the climate and lack of proper storage facilities. The governor's relief official

Danakil warrior standing guard over the U.S. AID relief grain shipped into the drought-ravaged tribal areas of Ethiopia. Much of the grain was spoiled and unfit for human consumption.

stated that the emergency relief food grain came in bulk and there was no place to store it.

I described the condition of the people waiting for grain. I explained that they told me they had been waiting for days in the cold.

There is no happy ending to this incident. The needy waited; the grain rotted in storage.

At other locations I observed tons and tons of emergency food grain in outside storage, unprotected or insufficiently protected, rotting, and so infested by insects as to be inedible, not even fit for animal consumption.

Grain for the Danakil tribes was rotting and worthless. Grain in Worenso and Eliwoha had been in outside storage more than two months and was rotting.

I inspected many grain storage areas, penetrating grain sacks with a testing probe, obtaining samples for analysis by the U.S. Department of Agriculture. The results were universal, obvious to the naked eye: The emergency food grain, stored in sacks on the bare ground, without protection under it, was rotten and infested with insects. It was spoiled and unfit to eat.

THE RAILROAD

The rail link between Ethiopia and the Afars and Issas port of Djibouti had been a source of much scandal. Railroad records indicated what was moved out of Ethiopia into Djibouti for export. Boxcars were being used to store grain, which compounded the problem. With so many of the cars used for storage, Ethiopia did not have enough rolling stock to run its railroad.

At Nazareth, I observed at least fifteen boxcars full of U.S. corn. No one could explain what was being done with that corn. Shipping agents in Djibouti reported on dishonesty involving one of the forwarding agents used by U.S. AID. Grain rolled into Ethiopia on the railroad; it rolled back again to Djibouti for reexport.

One shipping official identified five or six full railroad wagons that had come through with relief grain to be reexported and sold outside Ethiopia.

The young and the elderly were ravaged by Ethiopia's famine. Here they wait for grain distribution in Ethiopia's northern provinces.

Another shipping official at the port of Djibouti explained how the port was controlled and stated that the way crooked officials managed the reexport was to ship the grain out of Djibouti and then ship it back again. This official also explained that the Ethiopian military wanted the railroad wagons for troop movements, and diverted them from the emergency transport of grain.

ONE MASTER FOR ANOTHER

The totalitarian government of Haile Selassie fell in September 1974, in the midst of the famine. The new government was quick to exploit the evidence of the former government's corruption and injustices. But a decade later, in 1984, another cyclical drought occurred in the sub-Sahara region of Africa. The Marxist regime of Colonel Mengistu was at war with tribes in the north, in the provinces of Eritrea and Tigre, and in conflict with Somalia. When the drought struck, the Ethiopian government, which received $2.5 billion worth of weapons from the Soviet Union, sought contributions of food and relief supplies. Ethiopia began receiving millions of dollars from concerned donors, who were distressed by news photos of little children starving to death. From rock concerts to government assistance, the world responded to the new human crisis in Ethiopia. But nothing had changed. The pattern of injustice, deliberate starvation, and corruption was repeated.

Food supplies earmarked for the starving were blocked by Marxist government troops. Trucks shipped in to carry the food were, instead, used to carry troops to fight against the rebels in the north. In order to disperse populations friendly to the rebels, the Ethiopian government ordered forced death marches, "relocations," where refugees were made to trek long distances under the guns of soldiers.

In one situation, Australia shipped in 1 million dollars worth of food for famine relief. A ship carried 3,500 tons for Ethiopia and 6,000 tons for the starving in Sudan. The Ethiopian authorities seized and impounded the cargo, and denounced Australia in what the *New York Times* called a brazen charge "by a regime responsible for much of the misery others seek to alleviate."

Fleeing Marxist Ethiopia in 1986, Dawit Georgis, the former Ethiopian relief minister, requested and received asylum in the United States. Describing the abuse of power and the misuse of relief aid, Dawit confirmed American officials' worst fears.

In spite of the Ethiopian government's interference, people responded compassionately to this most recent famine. "We were given $50 million for Ethiopia," Lynn Marshall, of Catholic Relief Services, said. "Can you break the back of famine in Africa with money?" Lynn asked rhetorically. "No. Famine is more than the rains not coming. With all the talent and competency in New York City we cannot deal with the homeless in New York. We cannot cope with Park Avenue," Lynn said, gesturing out the window of his office in CRS's Church Center in Manhattan.

THE RELIEF FOOD ITSELF

Even with the goodwill of many dedicated people, many of the refugees could not digest the relief foods shipped in. Much of it, except the maize, was not compatible with the Ethiopian diet. Some concentrated powdered foodstuffs required special preparation before it could be used; some was just alien to the local diet.

Many relief supplies arrived without instructions on their use; some foods were incompatible with the Ethiopian diet. Hungry people ate some of the powders without preparation and many became sick.

Because instructions for use were missing, very expensive mixtures of corn and soya, for example, were not used correctly, with great waste resulting. When asked how the Ethiopians employed these specialized relief foods, the man in charge of the U.S. disaster program replied: "I don't know how they use it."

An American who had been living and working in Ethiopia for a long time said: "The Ethiopians don't eat these things. Most of it is rotted anyway. It's not even good to feed their animals."

The man shook his head. "They don't know what they're doing, these people. They don't care. The Ethiopian officials hope the famine kills their enemies. Everybody is stealing. Everybody knows they are stealing. It will be suppressed. The true scandal will never be brought to the eyes of the world. You won't do it. Your government won't let you. They knew everything but suppressed it." The man scoffed, laughed, then turned away so I couldn't see the tears in his eyes.

Tears also well up in the hollow eyes of mothers walking along the hunger road, desperately clinging to their skeletal children. Only mother love gives them the strength to go on, from nowhere to hopelessness. For the desperadoes in power—stealing, skimming, and profiteering from relief supplies—nothing has changed. Change is unlikely where starvation is big business. In spite of sympathy and human kindness, Ethiopian mothers still walk alone.

The agony on this mother's face is apparent as she carries her starving baby along the hunger road in Eritrea, in northern Ethiopia.

3
THE CONGO:
Revolution and Death

The feeding was so good in the Bukavu area that crocodiles moved upriver from Lake Tanganyika against a strong current to eat human corpses thrown in upstream. Congolese would not eat river fish for a long time because these fish had feasted off the lush pickings of unfortunate human victims. . . . The mercenaries were coolly efficient, well cut out for their job. They smiled wryly, describing the cadavers that used to float downriver. A couple of times the French-man, a mercenary . . . on the riverboat with his troops, kicked one of the big crocodiles tied on the lower deck, joking about how many victims of the rebellion the animal had probably finished off.

FROM NOTES MADE ON THE CONGO RIVER,
JULY 1966.

The way people of industrialized nations use the word *poor* has no application to the day-to-day lives of most African peoples. Their lives are tied to the environment. They farm to subsist; they hunt and fish and raise animals to live. If there is a bad harvest, if there is no catch, then they do not eat. If war, rebellion, or natural disaster disrupts their lives, their lands, or their daily food-gathering activities, then starvation takes its toll.

To call Africans who live in humble circumstances Third World people brings to mind a derogatory image of people living in squalor who do not care. In terms of the values of family harmony and devotion of members of a clan to one another, African peoples are

It is wrong to view people who live in developing countries as belonging to another world, a so-called Third World. Learning about other cultures and traditions can open unlimited horizons to human understanding.

very rich. The elderly have an important place in African culture, as do children, who rarely stray far from family guidance in their villages. But modern technology and communication have reached and affected the lives of tribal peoples, even those who live in the most remote African heartland without running water or electricity. To some degree this contact with the outside world has created a desire for another lifestyle; it has disrupted family life and tribal values.

The Congo that I saw when I was just out of my teens, working in mission hospitals, was part of this Africa in transition: torn by war and revolution, disrupted by greed and lust for outside values. It was a time when old ways were being thrown aside for new, and in the process great numbers of people suffered.

It is not called the Congo anymore. The names of most major cities, even the name of the vast river that courses through the nation, have been changed since I worked there in 1965 and 1966. Modern Zaire is a nation of some 32 million people living in an area nearly the size of the entire United States east of the Mississippi River, over a million and a quarter square miles. The more-than-250 tribes in Zaire are as different in custom and tradition as they are in their many languages. Even today, Zaire has a high infant mortality rate, topping 102 deaths per 1,000 live births, as well as serious health-care and nutrition problems.

Barely out of his teens, the author, John Fine, worked in mission hospitals in the Congo, helping to treat victims of starvation.

Zaire, the former Belgian Congo, then later called the Democratic Republic of the Congo, is a nation of bountiful natural resources. Yearly exports of almost 2 billion dollars worth of copper, petroleum, diamonds, coffee, manganese, and wood make it potentially one of the wealthiest countries in the world. In addition, Zaire produces 60 percent of the world's cobalt, which is used in the manufacture of aircraft. However, exploitation of this wealth by Belgium, the former colonial ruler, followed by the disruptions of revolution, fierce tribal warfare, and sectional fighting, have caused generation after generation of Congolese to suffer childhood malnutrition and starvation.

HISTORICAL PERSPECTIVE

Ancient peoples settled in the land that is now Zaire more than ten thousand years ago, leaving behind an anthropological record of their primitive civilization. In the seventh or eighth century A.D. Bantu tribes from an area that is present-day Nigeria settled and lived in Zaire. These tribes were cut off from outside influence until the Portuguese explored the mouth of the Congo River in 1482. It wasn't until Henry Stanley, a reporter for the *New York Herald*, traveled from East Africa to the mouth of the Congo River between 1874 and 1877 that the outside world glimpsed this area.

Belgian King Leopold II had commissioned Stanley to explore the Congo. As a result, at the Berlin Conference in 1885, King Leopold II was given the Zaire River Basin as his personal property. He ceded it to Belgium in 1907. The Congo proved a source of rich colonial exploitation for Belgium until unrest and riots in 1959 caused King Baudouin to grant it independence the following year.

The Belgians pulled out bitterly, reportedly sabotaging important public works facilities, for they were leaving behind a major source of wealth and national pride. Once the Belgians left, control degenerated, and peace lasted only one week. Warfare raged among various rebel factions who were inspired by communist infiltrators. Wholesale murder took place in conflicts that erupted between tribes whose longstanding animosities had been held in check only by Belgian troops.

At Stanleyville in the north, where the famous Stanley Falls makes the Congo River impassable, the rebels were winning. Thousands of people were murdered in brutal fighting and acts of terrorism. In order to quell the savage fighting, Belgian paratroopers were sent into Stanleyville. Jumping from U.S. Air Force planes, they liberated the city from the rebels.

Terrorism, murder, and atrocities were everywhere. The rebels with their mercenary officers were forced across the border into neighboring Angola in the south and into Rwanda in the north. But from their cross-border guerrilla camps, invasions and attacks continued through 1977 and 1978, fueled by outside interests that supplied arms and advisors.

THE CONGO IN CRISIS

Dr. Paul Carlson, a missionary physician, had been slain in Stanleyville (now called Kisangani) when the rebels attacked the city. As a consequence, whites were evacuated and the fledgling nation was left without adequate health care, medical supplies, and food. In the United States I learned about Dr. Carlson's murder, and his mission put me in touch with a church program still operating in the war-ravaged Congo. I obtained donations of medical supplies and drugs and set out for Africa. My first taste of what lay in store occurred on the airplane before we landed.

A soft-drink bottle exploded while a Pan Am stewardess was opening it, causing deep cuts in her leg. The plane landed in Leopoldville (now called Kinshasa) and the captain asked if anyone could provide first aid until they could get help, at their next stop. I told them I had my medical kit in the baggage, and it was brought out so I could use adhesive closures and antiseptic. While I was dressing the wound, the Pan Am ground crew said medical conditions in the Congo were crude and unsanitary and they did not want the stewardess treated there if at all possible.

Having bandaged her leg, I gathered up my baggage and disembarked on what would be a fascinating yet heart-rending experience, where disease, malnutrition, and hunger hung ominously over the people struggling for independence after long Belgian colonial rule.

Not far from the border between the Congo and Angola to the south, a panhandle of land containing the port of Matadi juts out into the ocean. Refugees from a violent struggle between Portuguese troops and rebels in nearby Angola were filtering over the border. Most of these refugees arrived in a deteriorated state of health, many of the children suffering from lack of protein in their diets, which results in the dread children's disease, kwashiorkor. This protein-deficiency disease is often irreversible; the children's bodies become swollen, their hair turns a rust-orange color and their skin peels off in large patches. Growth is retarded and they become listless; many internal organs begin to degenerate. It was here that I received my introduction to victims of poor diet and lack of proper health care in the Congo.

Elsewhere in the nation, communist-inspired rebels were fighting against poorly disciplined and badly trained national troops. To combat the insurgency, mercenaries were brought in to lead and train the Congolese soldiers. It was bad business. At the very best the mercenaries were antisocial brigands come to profit from what they could steal; worse, many were psychopathic killers whose cruelty and indifference to life made them feared wherever they went.

Through it all was the active participation by America's Central Intelligence Agency, which employed anti-Castro Cuban refugee pilots to fly missions out of Stanleyville against the rebels further to the north.

The nutritional crisis brought on by warfare was apparent. People with cases of chronic malnutrition streamed into the little dispensary. In their weakened, malnourished condition, children were susceptible to many diseases. Most suffered from malaria. Weakened by hunger, their frail little bodies were pathetic to see. Often they succumbed to minor ailments a healthy child could have overcome.

The hospital corridor was dark and I could see only the shadow of a little boy sitting alone on a wooden bench, waiting. I sat down

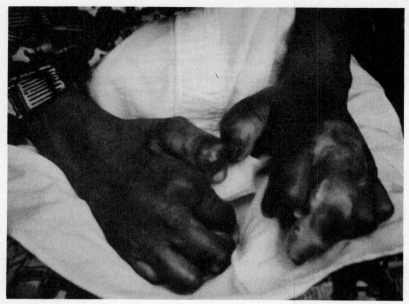

The author took a picture of this woman's hands before treating her. Unable to sense pain, lepers often hurt themselves over cooking fires, and the untreated wounds become infected.

next to him and asked what had happened and why he was waiting. The little boy motioned to his arm. I could not see it clearly in the dark corridor, except that it was wrapped in rags, so I asked him whether he hurt his arm playing with the other children.

"I am a leper," the little boy said, and my heart sank when I saw the hopelessness in his eyes.

Diseases that are known only in textbooks as curiosities in developed countries were rampant in the Congo. Leprosy is caused by long exposure to a bacteria that attacks the central nervous system, anesthetizing parts of the body. Victims often suffer horrible cuts and burns, unaware of the pain. Leprosy also attacks the cartilage in facial features. Ignorance of leprosy and fear of contagion from lepers has resulted in forced isolation and confinement of victims of this disease to colonies and camps.

Malaria, sleeping sickness, elephantiasis, and all manner of other tropical diseases and parasites also plagued the people of the Congo.

Only a dedicated handful of volunteers and medical missionaries, who had returned at great peril after independence, remained to help them.

A VISIT TO THE INTERIOR

As soon as it was reported to be safe, a Dutch nurse and I took a Land Rover and left the mission hospital in the south to visit rural dispensaries that had not received supplies nor the services of outside personnel since the rebel attacks started.

The roads were only muddy tracks; then even those pathways deteriorated and the four-wheel drive and winching cable, which could be attached to something stationary to pull the vehicle out, was in use most of the time as we traveled over the grueling but magnificent terrain of lush tropical forests into the interior.

We arrived in one village just as the people were about to celebrate in thanks for the cessation of hostilities and fighting. Our ve-

Women and children celebrate in the Congo to give thanks that the war had eased so they could soon return to their lives without fear or terror.

hicle was surrounded, and we could not drive on as villagers who had come to the little settlement from vast distances in the bush pressed in to touch me and the nurse. The welcome was overwhelming.

"If we had been here a few months ago, in this very place, these same people, under the influence of the rebels, would have killed us," the Dutch nurse told me in English, as I began to distribute little gifts I had brought for the children.

That thought refused to leave me and it has come back to me often since. The Dutch nurse's words, though I knew they were true, seemed incompatible with the spirit and warmth of these people, genuinely happy that we had come—a sign of deliverance, they said—with medical help for those in dire need.

That afternoon we set up our dispensary and the village elders sent word out into the bush that we had come. The evening was filled with celebrating, a meal shared with the elders. We were given the chieftain's hut to stay in. As light first began to filter through the thatch, I heard a quiet rustling outside, as though a small animal were browsing on the thatch. It was still barely light, so I turned over and slept again, until I was awakened by the heat of the new morning. There was still silence in the village; but when I opened the bamboo and thatch door to look outside the hut, the sight startled me.

During the night and early morning, hundreds of people had come. They had received word of the presence of medical missionaries in the village and they had walked, journeying long distances in the night to seek help. They came to have festering and infected wounds attended, to bring malnourished children; they traveled the jungle tracks, drawn by runners sent out with the message that there was hope.

We held clinic, using what medicines we had. The antibiotics that I had brought from the United States went quickly, antiseptic bottles emptied, and soon we were left with only jars of patent medicines, which had been part of the donations.

Many of the children and mothers we saw were suffering from vitamin deficiencies. In some cases, infants had been fed pap, a mixture of starchy food and water, because their mothers had been either unable or unwilling to breast-feed them. As a result the infants suffered malnutrition. Many were brought in from the bush with advanced protein deficiencies. The children's bones were fragile; in some cases they were in critical condition, unable to fight off relatively minor colds.

Some patients we saw had been treated by shamans. Mothers still clasped amulets and potions that had been prepared for their children. Superstition and ignorance, coupled with lack of proper food and medical attention, claimed many lives.

One harmless and rather comic example of the kind of superstition that surrounded medicine in this part of Africa occurred toward the end of clinic as evening fell, when a man arrived pointing to wounds he had received when he fell from his bicycle and slid down a hill. I cleaned the deep scratches. Where he complained of bruises and aches, I applied Vicks Vapo Rub from a jar in the now nearly empty medical kit. For the injured man, this was strong medicine; the smell and effect of the pomade, used normally to relieve minor aches or as an inhalant breathed through a vaporizer when one has a cold, convinced him of its worth. The man turned and pointed to his cut lip and tongue and motioned to the scratches on his face and arms.

I told him no; I explained in French through the Congolese interpreter who translated my words into Kikongo, that it would burn and wasn't for use on open cuts. There was an animated discussion among the Congolese in the dispensary. When the interpreter spoke to me again in French he said that I would have to apply the Vicks Vapo Rub as the man wanted. The interpreter explained that the man was a very important man in the clan and was not to be refused this strong medicine. I told the interpreter to tell the man that it would hurt. After he spoke to the injured man, the interpreter told me again that the pain was no matter and I was to apply the medicine.

I rubbed a small amount of the Vicks on the man's lip first, gently. It hurt, since the cut was open. In the Congolese way of expressing

pain, the man snapped his fingers while shaking his wrist. He refused
to let me stop, sticking out his tongue, pointing to the cut, and he
had me apply the pomade to his other wounds. The injured man
wouldn't leave until he was allowed to have a large scoop of the Vapo
Rub to take with him, assuring everyone in the village that these
foreigners had brought good medicine and were good people.

THE MERCENARIES

If I had been older during my time in the Congo, perhaps I would
have seen things in a different light, been more aware of the danger.
What I might have approached with prudence later on seemed an
adventure at the time. Thus, I was not overly cautious when I arrived
in Stanleyville soon after the rebel forces had been driven out of the
city and it was being held by white mercenaries—men from
Rhodesia (now Zimbabwe), France, South Africa, and Belgium.
(The Belgians were part of a Technical Assistance program.)

Spent cartridges were everywhere. Buildings had been machine-
gunned and were full of bullet holes. The American Embassy had
sent a man in to check on the consulate. When I saw him in the
ransacked office trying to recover documents strewn about he complained that the mercenaries used the light fixtures for target practice. I saw the walk-in safe where whites had hidden from the Simba
rebels who killed Dr. Carlson, locking themselves inside until relief
forces freed them.

As I walked about Stanleyville, evidence of the fighting was everywhere. In the distance along the dirt track, I saw a man pedaling a
bicycle. He was coming toward me. I could not make out what it
was he had tied behind the seat. As he passed, I smiled and the man
waved, glassy eyed, but with a momentary smile. I turned to look
after him as he passed me and saw a small wooden infant's coffin tied
on behind him.

Terrorist activity and fighting disrupted people's daily lives and
their ability to feed themselves. Even fishing in the river was danger-
ous, and there were many reports of atrocities on local people. Some
families, desperate for food, chanced fishing despite the peril of

attack from rebels, their own national army troops, or the mercenaries brought in to help quell the rebellion. These paid foreign soldiers showed no mercy to the poor in their daily quest for food to nourish their families. The mercenaries were cold, without emotion. They told me about entering villages, spraying bullets everywhere; for them it didn't matter whom they killed. One young French mercenary with mean eyes, squinting so that the yellow circles around their green iris gave him a sinister look, described how the bodies of Congolese killed in the rebellion floated downriver, so thick at times, the mercenaries said, that they blocked their patrol boat. Thousands more died from starvation, refugees without food, without hope.

Crocodiles, a readily available food source and considered a delicacy in the Congo, had been loaded aboard a riverboat I boarded with mercenary officers and Congolese soldiers in Stanleyville. Croco-

The white mercenary refused to pose for a picture, apparently a wanted man hiding from the law. The Congolese soldier knelt down by the large crocodile the mercenary had just kicked, commenting about how many victims of the revolution the animal had eaten.

diles were transported alive, their jaws tied shut, legs tied to a long pole that was used to sling the animals between two men when they were carried. A couple of times the French mercenary kicked one of the large crocodiles tied to the lower deck, cruelly joking about how many victims of the rebellion the animal had finished off.

In the east, mercenaries told me that feeding was so good on cadavers in the Bukavu area that crocodiles moved up river from Lake Tanganyika against a strong current to feed on the human corpses thrown in upstream. The mercenaries joked, telling how the Congolese wouldn't eat fish from the river because they had feasted on human victims.

In the north, as soon as some semblance of order was restored, the preindependence ordinance requiring that the skin be left on animals sold at market was enforced when it was discovered that human meat was being sold, so desperate were the people for food.

Atrocity after atrocity occurred with the breakdown of social order after independence. In my notes I observed: "Gaunt and hungry refugees, swollen with edema and vitamin deficiency, straggle into the dispensaries in search of help. Many have lost all sense of caring and accept whatever is done to them. They come three times abused: maltreated by the enemy, the mercenaries, and their own soldiers. They die from starvation and lack of medical attention; many die in the bush, never reaching help at all. Estimates of the dead reach as high as two million. Countless numbers will always bear the scars of fear and terror."

Because I wore medical whites, the mercenaries on board the riverboat with me knew I was attached to a mission hospital. The Frenchman said their medical officer had been killed, and they would take me off the riverboat at the military camp downriver to serve in place of their doctor. I knew better than to refuse, but told them that I was expected back at the hospital. They considered the discussion ended and told me I would be paid two thousand dollars a month.

In the days that followed, as the boat churned along with the river current, we talked about many things. When the boat snagged on sandbars, the mercenaries checked their machine guns to be sure they were ready in the event of attack from rebels who infiltrated the river on either side.

The impenetrable jungle, the sights and sounds of the country, and the day-to-day life on shipboard were fascinating to me. As we sat at table to eat on the last night before the mercenaries and their contingent of soldiers were to disembark, the Frenchman said they would not take me off; they would let me continue downriver. The Frenchman later put a mark on my cabin door so that the troops that would be put aboard to ride the boat the rest of the way to the capital would not bother me.

The next morning as I watched the mercenaries shoulder their heavy automatic weapons and walk down the gangplank, I wondered about the future of Africa and its people. Certainly the days of colonial rule were numbered, but in the transfer of power, would the people experience more cruelty than they could ever conceive of? Would the voices of those who would stand to gain most in the division of this new power and wealth be heard above the people's cries for peace?

A FRAGILE PEACE

A fragile peace has come to Zaire. There is still fighting and cross-border sorties. The U.S. Central Intelligence Agency and Zaire's Service of Military Action and Reconnaissance continue to supply arms to Unita (Union for the Total Independence of Angola) rebels fighting to overthrow Angola's Marxist government. The arms are supplied through a 1986 15 million-dollar U.S. aid budget for Unita. Gun shipments have reportedly been flown into Angola from airstrips in Zaire. Military aid to Zaire from the United States amounted to almost 11 million dollars in 1986 and 1987.

There is a terrible price to be paid for all this arms trafficking. Jan van Hoogstraten, the former head of Church World Service's Africa Department and one of the most experienced Africa experts in the

world, said: "America must be convinced to stop supplying these
African nations with arms. I see it all the time. Sophisticated weapons are used by Africans to kill Africans."

For the people of Zaire, who must farm and fish each day to
supply their basic needs, peace is the most important commodity.
Tropical diseases and malnutrition claim the lives of too many victims even in the best of times. The world must be aware of the
tragedy war and rebellion have already played in this new nation and
work through diplomacy to insure peace.

The Congo River, now called the Zaire River, is rich in fish. During the revolution,
Simba rebels terrorized the civilian population, disrupting their normal food gathering
activities. Driven from their homes, the people starved.

4

THE SAHEL:
Disaster in the Desert

I left the embassy compound in Mali feeling sick. By the time I reached Senegal I was shaking with fever. I piled all the blankets I could find over me. Although the outside temperature was 135 degrees, I still trembled under the blankets. The fever made me delirious. Malaria comes in cycles; that night I was able to arise and catch a flight to the United States. I spent a week in hospital drifting in and out of consciousness, longer recuperating at home. Fits of malaria still come back when my resistance is low. I can understand the plight of the African firsthand.

REFLECTIONS AFTER HOSPITAL STAY WITH
MALARIA CAUGHT IN MALI WHILE ON MISSION
WITH THE STATE DEPARTMENT INVESTIGATING
EFFECTS OF THE DROUGHT.

It is a belt across Africa, below the Sahara Desert and above the well-watered range of tropical Africa. This area, called the Sahel, is roughly four thousand miles long and about one thousand miles wide. The same sort of terrain, in fact, forms a belt across and around Earth in the latitude between the tenth and twentieth parallels. Drought in this zone has been felt in the Maharashtra Province of India, through the Yangtze Valley in China, and into the same latitude in Central America. In the Sahel, around the waist of Africa, drought has become a disaster in the desert.

The word *Sahel* is Arabic; it means *shore,* and has been applied to regions of Mauritania, Mali, Niger, Upper Volta, Chad, the

The desert, vast and unrelenting, encroaching on the Sahel, the midsection of Africa, where people managed to eke out a subsistence over centuries. Much of the world is an unarable desert where food is sparse.

Sudan, and the Central African Republic. Parts of Senegal, Dahomey (Benin), Kenya, and Tanzania were affected by drought conditions in the Sahel region, as was Ethiopia, which we have already discussed.

The desert moves south, bringing drought, drying up water holes, and turning what is marginal land, where nomads, subsistance farmers, and herdspeople are barely able to eke out enough to survive in the best of times, into a land of little hope.

The situation in the Sahel provoked Richard Jolly, Deputy Executive Director of UNICEF, the United Nation's Children's Fund, to say, "The most extreme situation is that in Africa, where the disaster of drought follows a decade or more of misdirected development, national and international, and has pushed some thirty million persons to the extremes of hunger, starvation, and often death."

The UNICEF program director's remarks have been underscored by the World Bank, which estimates that there are 100 million malnourished Africans, 20 million more than in 1980.

THE LAND AND THE DILEMMA

Along the Sahel belt where the Sahara encroaches, this band of marginal land where rainfall fluctuations have caused drought conditions over history, live the nomadic people of Africa: tribes of proud travelers in the desert who come and go, remaining in one place only long enough to find forage for their animals. Many of these nomadic people recognize no national boundaries, living as their ancestors have lived for centuries. The people and their nomadic lifestyles are suited to the land and the environment. Their cattle, camels, and goats are their only wealth, their currency and means of exchange as well as their pride and heritage. Some settlers live in hamlets and villages along this shore, this Sahel, this borderland where the desert encroaches and where nature has tempted life into a place where few would choose to survive.

In normal times, rainfall in the Sahel belt of sub-Sahara Africa varies within a range of about 20 percent of the norm. This enables the people to adapt their agriculture to the conditions and continue

Nomads with their caravans lived for thousands of years in the desert. When the drought came, their herds were decimated and their way of life imperiled.

to produce food grains to supply their needs when there is less rain.

History records great droughts in the Sahel, periods in which the monsoon rains didn't come or there was too little rainfall. One such catastrophe occurred in 1913, causing death and disaster. In recent times, drought struck the region in the early seventies, then again a decade later in the eighties.

Just what climatic and environmental conditions are responsible for the rains' not coming to the Sahel are not precisely known. There is a theory that freezing polar air, which recedes to the north in spring and summer, draws temperate air masses behind it, bringing moist air and the monsoon rains to the Sahel. As winter approaches, polar air masses begin their southerly migration and the dry season returns to the Sahel.

It has been suggested that these polar air masses have been affected by Earth's changing temperature and have not been receding as far into the north in spring and summer. Therefore, temperate air that brings the rains to the Sahel has not been following them as far north, either.

Whether this meteorological theory is true or not, we have seen significant changes in the temperature and climate of Earth in recent years. When the drought struck in the Sahel region in 1972, rainfall dropped to less than 70 percent of the norm. This was far below the ability of the fragile agricultural system of the region to respond. In one year the desert advanced more than sixty miles. Villages and settlements, whose residents had barely managed to survive before the drought by planting sorghum and millet, became ghost towns. Sand blew across the arid land, covering the crops.

In one city in Mauritania's Sahel belt, normal rainfall measures 200 millimeters. In 1973, the second year of acute drought in the region, only 41.6 millimeters fell. Animals died or were sold as the people from the marginal desert areas fled to cities, which could not cope with the influx of refugees.

Programs and policies that had been put in place to help these people survive on their marginal lands proved to be their undoing. A crisis unfolded, leaving brutal testimony to well-intentioned but misguided attempts to adjust nature to human needs. Various aid projects undertook well drilling to supply water in the region, and some 1,400 wells were dug in the Sahel. Human and animal health-care programs brought into the region encouraged permanent settlement on land in the Sahel with increased herds.

There had been reason to be optimistic. Good rainfall had come in the sixties. The desert was turned into pasture, and nomads and subsistence farmers were tempted by the prospects of good crops, foreign aid, and imported technology. Wells pumped by hand limit the amount of water a herdsman can draw for his cattle. With the motor-driven pumps brought in by foreign assistance, it was possible to pump more water and keep more cattle.

When the drought came, as it was bound to, the delicate environmental balance that might have enabled the people to survive through the hardship had been upset by the misguided development; death and disaster followed. The expanded population in the

Africans in a village in Angola use a UNICEF-supplied hand pump. *(UNICEF photo by Maggie Murray-Lee)*

region was decimated. Carcasses of dead animals littered the sand near dried-up water holes. It is difficult to tally the toll in human terms. Estimates say thousands were killed by starvation and disease brought on by malnutrition and unsanitary conditions. Thousands of square miles of land were reclaimed by the desert.

The tragedy that occurred in the seventies was repeated a decade later. Lessons from the earlier catastrophe should have educated aid workers, developers, and planners to the problems of adjusting nature to suit human purpose.

Ten years after the disaster of the seventies, the media mobilized again. The fashionable and hip focused on suffering and death. Rock bands raised money for relief, while foreign aid critics bemoaned programs that had failed to prevent another disaster in the desert. The bottom line remained the same: The fragile ecosystems that had supported life in the region had been disrupted, compounding a tragedy, crushing expectations, destroying human dreams.

The pattern of developmental disaster and institutional interference in the Sahel region, coupled with a great deal of incompetence and impropriety in responding to the tragedy of human starvation, offers an important opportunity to learn about the environment and human nature.

RELIEF IN THE SEVENTIES

America provided about 241 million dollars worth of food and drought relief assistance in central and west Africa between 1973 and 1975. Of this, approximately 109 million dollars went to Senegal, Mali, Mauritania, and Gambia. How the money was spent, whether the food reached the needy, and the long-term effect of the development projects are important questions that will be explored here.

Though there are many examples of poor planning, waste, even corruption and political misconduct, food and medicine that eventually reached the needy did help to stave off starvation and disease and saved lives. However, by the time the world bureaucracy was motivated and food and supplies for relief arrived in the Sahel, it was too late for the field workers to effectively plan distribution. There are few roads in the area, most are merely dirt tracks, and rail links are sparse. In many cases the food planners took so long that by the time relief supplies were ready to roll, the summer monsoons had come, flooding what roads there were, making it impossible to travel into the interior.

The United Nations Food and Agricultural Organization, while knowing that timely shipment of donated foods was of primary importance, was slow to act. Many weeks were wasted before decisions were made. Some shipments arrived in such large quantities that transport and storage capacity of the ports were overloaded. Food spoiled, became infested by pests, or was eaten by rats. At other times shipments arrived in too-small quantities, wasting the transport that had been ready to move it out to the needy areas.

In the Darfur region of Sudan, wheat donated by the U.S. is loaded onto rafts to be transported across the wadi, a gorge that floods after heavy rains. *(UNICEF photo by Maria Antonietta, Peru)*

In Niger, where it required five weeks to move the food from the ports to the interior where the needy waited, food arrived, in 1973, after the rains had closed the roads, so an airlift had to be undertaken. The futility of bad planning and poor implementation of relief efforts prompted Niger's then-president Hamani Diori to complain, as reported in the *New York Times,* "The international community spent over 40 million dollars on transporting food to Niger last year. Most of that money went on the airlift. For that kind of money we could have irrigated 11,000 hectares of land near the Niger River, which would have produced 110,000 tons of food. That is not far from our total needs."

In Chad, airplanes were using nineteen tons of fuel to deliver one ton of relief supplies. In Mali, the U.S. Air Force used one ton of fuel for every ton of food it airlifted from the capital, Bamako, to Gao in the north.

Many expensive items were being supplied to Sahel nations by the U.S. Agency for International Development (AID), disregarding field conditions. In one example, most of a fleet of thirty-six U.S.-

made trucks supplied for use in Mali were out of service, beyond repair. The trucks were designed for use on roads with hard surfaces. Half a million dollars was spent on vehicles unsuited for the region. In Senegal the same thing occurred. Many of the one hundred American-supplied vehicles were consigned to a scrap yard, testimony to poor planning and waste of resources.

U.S. AID relief assistance also was furnished to Gambia, a small coastal nation surrounded by Senegal with a population of 500,000. Between 1968 and 1972, Gambia's foreign exchange reserves increased from 6 to 10 million dollars. With a spectacular harvest of groundnuts, peanuts, and the like, and high export prices, Gambia, by September 30, 1974, had 32 million dollars in hard foreign exchange. The country had ample hard foreign currency to help any of its citizens who may have suffered the effects of the drought. Yet U.S. AID continued to supply relief food grains to Gambia, even after it was clear that none were needed.

To Senegal, U.S. AID supplied 18,600 metric tons of food grains,

In Mali, U.S. AID-supplied trucks were unsuited to the terrain. They quickly became unusable, cadavers in a junkyard, memorials to the best intentions gone awry.

which cost $3.8 million. Senegal didn't need it. At the end of 1974, Senegal was able to organize an International Trade Fair, which cost 40 million dollars, prompting an international body to report Senegal "will no doubt be in a position to afford about 5 percent of that amount for assistance to drought and pest-affected population groups in parts of the country, taking into consideration that the food resources needed can be mobilized in the country itself."

Investigation of UNICEF's management of the distribution of 500 tons of corn-soya-milk donated by the United States in 1974, revealed that inaction by the government of Mauritania in spite of UNICEF's protests resulted in waste and spoilage. In Gambia, UNICEF distributed the U.S.-donated corn-soya-milk to relief centers already receiving it through Catholic Relief Services programs.

In another program the United States regularly contributed 250 metric tons of vegetable oil for cooking to countries that export 200,000 metric tons of peanut oil each year. Peanut oil is perfectly good for cooking and is used for that purpose by the people of the region. This is another example of improper allocation of relief resources.

In Senegal a more than 2-million-dollar livestock-range project and cattle program was planned. Not only was the project undertaken without a basic understanding of the relationship of the animals to their environment, but it was done with no notion of animal husbandry.

The range project proposed that cattle be kept in a watershed area all year long. Not only would the area be cut off in the rainy season, but the lush, watery grass the cattle would eat on the range-project land would cause them to lose body weight. Cattle must eat some dry grass or dry feed to gain weight. During the rainy season, ticks and flies, which transmit diseases to cattle and cause severe bites, abound in the area set aside for the range project. The herdsmen's normal patterns for grazing their cattle is to move them north in the rainy season, then south in the dry season.

Just these few examples make it clear that relief efforts in the Sahel were poorly coordinated and badly planned. When there are people who need food and food is wasted or sent where it is not needed, when rehabilitation projects are poorly planned, environmentally unsound, and so flawed that in the long run they do more harm than good, then the people being helped are often left worse off than before.

THE SAHEL IN THE EIGHTIES

Millions of dollars were spent to relieve the crisis caused by drought in the seventies. The immediate disaster passed; rains came. Bureaucrats prospered as governmental relief agencies beefed up staffs previously reduced by layoffs and austerity cuts. Foreign relief organizations geared up to spend money earmarked for relief and rehabilitation, implementing medium- and long-range development projects they said would prevent future disasters in the region. In 1984, the rains failed again. The tragedy that befell the people in the Sahel region in the early seventies was repeated.

In a region of Mauritania hard hit by the 1973 drought, 1984 rainfall was measured at 25 to 30 percent of the average taken over the forty-year period before 1972. Wheat, sorghum, and other grain production fell dramatically. Mauritania had recovered after the 1973 disaster. Farmers were producing an annual yield of some 100,000 tons of grains. But in 1984, only 16,000 tons were produced, about 6 percent of the nation's grain needs.

In Mauritania's Sahel region, in 1985, laborers worked to clear away sand that covered the main road as winds swept the desert south. Refugees flocked to the edge of the road, calling it the Road of Hope; they waited, squatters camped in tents and shanties seeking free food and water. These refugees were once proud nomads, herdspeople whose lives were tied to the timelessness of shifting desert sands. Now they waited for free food and water; some of them were survivers of the drought ten years earlier.

In Chad, the desert advanced 125 miles, affecting the lives of half the population. In Upper Volta, little had changed except the name of the country, now called Burkina Faso. Alan Cowell of the *New York Times* interviewed a man in Burkina Faso who had come

A mother and her two children wait by the side of the Road of Hope in Mauritania. *(UNICEF photo)*

through the drought in the seventies. The refugee told him, "I am in my fifty-fourth year of life but I have never seen a year like this. This year is worse than 1973, because then we could sell cattle. The markets have disappeared. After many years of drought, people have nothing to sell."

Were the patterns of life of the nomadic people of Africa so disrupted that they could no longer survive in their environment? Had the influences of foreign aid and government interference, which changed the patterns of their lives, compounded the natural disaster so as to make it impossible for them to return to their former way of life? These questions were not academic for the Africans waiting for food along the roadsides. The desert, once their home, was now their enemy. They fled, displaced persons, perhaps never to return to a way of life that had kept their people alive for three thousand years.

Proud nomads have become citizens of poverty camped out along the hunger road waiting for the dole of free food; stripped of a way of life. They had been set up by policies attributed to progress, then struck down by nature.

The same problems that beset relief efforts in the seventies befell relief efforts in the eighties. War and religious and tribal animosities once again interfered.

In the Sudan, for example, war between Moslem government forces and Christian rebels stopped relief shipments. A United Nations convoy bringing food to almost a million drought-affected people in the Sudan was blocked by the rebels in 1985.

In the typical patterns of the region, the drought was followed by torrential rainfall. The problem of reaching the drought-affected population in the Sudan was then compounded by flooding that washed out bridges and roads. The "solution" used in the seventies was repeated: U.S. AID employed military helicopters to airlift food into the Sudan, a costly way of dealing with relief when timely action and planning could have predicted and managed the problem before it became a disaster.

The underlying reasons for the human tragedy in the Sudan

Masai herdsmen tend their cattle. The drought in the Sahel decimated the herds, forcing these proud people to become refugees.

followed a pattern evident throughout the Sahel. Development undertaken without consideration of the environment had caused the collapse of the fragile ecology. There were too many people settled on lands unable to support them. Government interference with indigenous agricultural production and market pricing changed the way the agricultural system had functioned for centuries. When the drought came, its impact was hardest on the nomads and seminomadic settlers whose lives had been altered by great expectations—false expectations based on bad developmental decisions. These people had survived over history by adapting their lifestyles to nature and natural forces. This prompted the World Bank to report in 1985 that the "basic cause of Africa's troubles was misguided policies followed by governments in the past that wasted resources and discouraged farming and private business."

There were serious mistakes and deliberate misconduct; some of the responsibility for the tragedy must be shared by the people whose expectations tempted them to be greedy. But blame has no meaning in the face of even one suffering child. The worldwide outpouring of human kindness in response to the crisis in the eighties has no parallel in history.

LIVE AID

An Irish pop musician saw firsthand the crisis of starving children in Africa. As a result, he motivated rock musicians to donate time for a massive benefit performance known as Live Aid. The results were overwhelming. Thousands of young people joined with their

People gather outside mission stations and UNICEF-assisted feeding centers for food and other essential materials. The villages where they used to live have become completely deserted because of a combination of looting, cattle raiding, and severe drought. *(UNICEF photo by Arild Vollan)*

elders to donate money during a sixteen-hour marathon performance in Britain. Also donated in the United Kingdom and the United States were the profits from hit songs. Money from "Do They Know It's Christmas?" went to Live Aid, and Grammy-Award-winning "We Are the World" profits went to USA for Africa. These efforts raised 100 million dollars for African relief.

Bob Geldof, Live Aid's organizer, worked tirelessly to motivate donors as well as governments in Africa to do something about the crisis. While his career is popular music, Bob Geldof confided, "Pop music is a pretty unimportant thing." This reaction is a common one of people who have witnessed the effects of hunger on children. Seeing the desperation and suffering of fellow human beings puts a new perspective on what is really important in life.

Being unconventional, at times confronting and challenging government officials and heads of state in front of world television cameras, has earned Bob Geldof a reputation as Live Aid's bad boy. He often puts officials on the spot to urge their help in famine relief. Bob makes no apology for his irreverent conduct. "When you have an absolute moral certainty that what you're doing saves people from suffering, then it's right," Geldof declared.

Through their music, which was sung and played while films of starving children were projected, these musicians reached the hearts of millions. Their actions prove that a few people, regardless of their age or position, can make a difference. It only requires determination and commitment.

The responses of governments to the latest African drought was also overwhelming. The United States spent 590 million dollars for African famine relief in 1985 and pledged another 411 million dollars worth of food aid, bringing the total spent for African famine victims to over 1 billion dollars. Thirteen industrial nations and the World Bank pledged another 1.1 billion dollars, establishing a Special Facility for Sub-Sahara Africa. This money, to be administered by the World Bank, was designed to aid countries that agree to change practices that World Bank experts see as the causes of the African disaster. The World Bank imposed conditions on these

Innocent mothers and children suffer in Uganda in an environment where moral and economic values have been destroyed. *(UNICEF photo by Arild Vollan)*

funds requiring African nations receiving them to adopt policies that eliminate bureaucracy, waste, and abuse; and implement plans to assist farmers and agriculture; and to encourage private businesses and free enterprise.

The 100 million dollars raised by Band Aid and Live Aid is being used not only to relieve famine and feed the hungry in the Sahel and Ethiopia, but to fund sound long-term development projects. The amount of this assistance is staggering; whether it will accomplish the permanent good its well-intentioned donors hope for is unknown.

That food and famine relief in the eighties was abused and misused, just as it was in the seventies, is clear. Alan Cowell, the writer for the *New York Times* who investigated the problem, reported, "Nothing is more politicized than statistics of food. Governments inflate their needs, base their calculations on exaggerated criteria in individual food requirements to mask their own shortcomings, and feed for free those whose needs are not so great but who have a political significance. Or profit may be made on food given by those in the west whose farmers have grown a surplus in need of a market."

There is a cynical reality in what Cowell writes, a cynical truth in what he observed in Africa, what many observed. There is, of course, tremendous waste, so much waste and fraud and abuse in foreign aid programs that it shocks the human conscience when we know children are dying for want of a little food.

Perhaps Bob Geldof put it best when he confronted Britain's Prime Minister Margaret Thatcher in front of television cameras. Geldof asked the prime minister to supply surplus butter for famine relief. The prime minister replied that Africans cannot use the butter, that they cannot eat it. Geldof countered that butter can be converted to butter oil, which Africans can consume.

Frustrated, unable to get the pop musician to accept her point of view, caught in an embarrassing situation while television cameras filmed the impromptu exchange, Prime Minister Thatcher said fi-

Children in part of the affected region of Tanzania dress in traditional garb.

nally, "There is no simple answer," trying to back away from the confrontation.

The young pop musician, known for his disheveled hair and ragged jeans, managed to get in the last word. "Nothing is as simple as dying, Prime Minister," Bob Geldof countered, making any other comment seem immaterial.

5
ASIA:
The Hunger Road

Xenophobic. I didn't have to go look the word up. In his next breath the embassy bureaucrat explained: They dislike foreigners. If I had given any credence to the label, I might have failed in my mission among these proud, fiercely independent, and extremely warm people. Labels make people less than human; it is easy to disregard a Gook or a Geek, a Zip or a Slope. The Afghanis have great courage and substance. They will need friends; trouble is coming their way.

NOTES MADE IN AFGHANISTAN PRIOR TO THE
RUSSIAN INVASION.

Asia is a vast continent with many different people. There are 1 billion 50 million people in China alone, 104 million in Bangladesh, 785 million in India, 102 million in Pakistan. These most recent figures from the Population Reference Bureau were outdated before they were even tabulated and are millions short as they are read here.

What can be said in one chapter, in one book, in an encyclopedia, or in a library of books that will have any significance about an area so large? What can be said about a population almost uncountable, peoples so different, problems whose dimensions seem to have no boundaries, about a region where hunger, malnutrition, disease, and poverty are taken for granted?

What we can and will do is to introduce the people and their problems, try to touch on major issues, and sow seeds that you, the

future planners and movers of power on this planet, can reap to help
the hungry—seeds of knowledge and concern for the future, a future
in which Asia will surely play an important role.

AFGHANISTAN

About 15.4 million people live, or lived, in a country roughly the size
of Texas, about 260,000 square miles. Today, close to 3 million
Afghan refugees have sought asylum in Pakistan and another million
have fled to Iran and the west. The Russians came in force on
December 24, 1979, and have remained with 120,000 troops. There
was fighting in all of the twenty-nine Afghan provinces. The Soviets
have left, but their surrogate regime remains in power.

In Afghanistan a puppet regime established by the Russians was unable to cope with
proud resistance by people whose religion and independence demanded they be free.
The Russians invaded, destroying farms and livestock, hoping to force the people
into submission.

Afghanistan came under the Soviet sphere of influence more because of geography than from necessity. It is a landlocked country bordering Russia, Pakistan, Iran, and China. The mountainous nation has always been known for its fierce warriors. Alexander the Great invaded in 328 B.C. The Arabs invaded in A.D. 642, bringing Islam.

In 1219, the Mongols under Genghis Khan laid waste to the civilization, destroying and sacking the cities. After the death of Genghis Khan, petty chiefs ruled until the late fourteenth century, when Khan's descendant, Tamerlane, brought Afghanistan into the Asian empire he had created.

Modern Afghanistan was founded in 1747 by Ahmad Shah Durani, who ruled from Meshed to Kashmir and Delhi and from the northern Oxus River to the Arabian Sea. A succession of foreign rulers attempted to control the nation. Each time, fierce resistance fighters created such havoc that the foreigners capitulated.

Mohammad Daud, Afghanistan's prime minister, overthrew the monarchy and seized power in 1973, courting military aid from the Russians. Daud was assassinated in 1978 in a violent coup that established a Marxist government in Kabul, the capital. By December 1978, the Russians had signed a new pact with the Afghan government and military assistance escalated to maintain the puppet regime.

With the Soviet invasion, the will to resist increased and the resistance fighters took to the mountains with rifles and small arms, holding the heavily armed Russian troops and tanks at bay.

It is this fighting, and the deliberate disruption of agriculture in rebel areas by the Russians, that have caused and compounded human suffering among the Afghan people.

Fighting in rugged mountain terrain, the fierce Afghan warriors with their flowing mustaches and flaming eyes, daggers at their sides, ancient and well-worn rifles slung over their shoulders, seem like figures from romantic legends. Rifles against tanks, swords against helicopters, steep mountain passes where only donkeys can trod, partisans slipping arms and ammunition across the border from

The rugged mountains and terrain in Afghanistan protected small bands of resistance fighters who would ambush Russian convoys, often with muskets made well over a hundred years ago.

Pakistan: This is the stuff of great adventure. The adventure in Afghanistan unfolds not on the pages of a novel, nor on a Hollywood movie set, but in remote villages where unsanitary rural conditions, lack of medicine, and food shortages make life tenuous for the people who live there.

In the capital, Kabul, and in the villages, open sewers run through the streets carrying contagion and disease. The lack of hygienic conditions of the water and food is responsible for spreading disease and infection, and with the war, even the rudimentary public health services that existed before the Russian invasion have broken down.

The winter snows block passes and roads; if villagers and members of family settlements have not been able to harvest enough food, or if their herds have not been kept safe, they will starve. There are no supermarkets, merely a primitive food system that depends on agriculture to feed the people through the winters.

Those refugees in Pakistan who have fled the fighting are being helped, but the influx of refugees has already strained the ability of Pakistan's resources and the resources of the United Nations and private voluntary organizations working in the border region. The refugees that have fled to Iran face a nation where internal revolution and bloody war with Iraq make it unlikely that they will receive much help.

In the streets of Kabul, open sewers cause unsanitary conditions in the market area, where women shop for food for their families.

There will be books inspired by the Afghan resistance, a conflict that will end now the Russians have decided that the cost is too great to stay. The cost will be measured in military terms; the final assessment of courage, in romantic terms; but for the suffering children, who die quietly, unnoticed, coughing until a frail heart gives out, there is no roll of honor, no military parade, no requiem.

Afghan children mind their cattle along a mountain stream.

INDIA

Holding a desperately ill child, so tiny that its wrinkled body almost fits in the palm of one of her strong hands, her other hand cupped around the baby's head, a small, aged Roman Catholic nun gives the infant a last moment of comfort before it dies. She is a sister to the sick, a parent to abandoned children, and she provides hospice to the terminally ill; hers is the last human voice heard before the abandoned die.

Her view of population declares a universal truth of human love. "Children should be a joy, a pleasure," Mother Teresa says. To those who would debate issues about population control with her, she answers, "Why are people so worried about world population? There is plenty of land in India for people to live on. It is so rich a country."

There is simple truth in what she says, yet the practice of this truth is so far from application that one must wonder why having enough land to grow food on, enough resources to feed and house the desperate in India, have not made it so. Why has not the *ahimsa,* the Hindu and Buddhist positive inner virtue that cares for the welfare of all, made it so?

Mahatma Gandhi did intellectual battle with the poverty and injustice in his country, offering an important insight about the dole. "My *ahimsa* would not tolerate the idea of giving a free meal to a healthy person who has not worked for it in some honest way and, if I had the power, I would stop every *sadavrata* [free distribution of meals]. . . . It has degraded the nation and it has encouraged laziness, idleness, hypocrisy and even crime. . . . Do not say you will maintain the poor on charity," Gandhi declared.

We have launched a discussion of the problems of poverty and hunger in India with two salvos. But what introduction could have more relevance than the words of Mother Teresa and Gandhi? Human suffering and a reflection on a history of aid that has failed to come to grips with the underlying problems of the vast population of this country twice the size of Alaska, over a million and a quarter square miles.

India's cities are burgeoning: New Delhi has 5.2 million people;

An open sewer runs through the middle of this densely populated slum in a village in India. Poor sanitation and hygiene cause many diseases. *(UNICEF photo by Sean Sprague)*

Calcutta, 9 million; and Bombay, 8 million. Crowded into hovels, lost on the streets, begging, pulling themselves through the gutters, deformed by disease, without hope, India's cities are cesspools of suffering for the poor.

A BRIEF HISTORY

India has existed as a civilization since 2500 B.C. Arab influence expanded into the area in the seventh and eighth centuries A.D., then a Moslem dynasty of the Mogul Empire ruled the area. The British established an outpost in India in 1619, controlled by the East India

Company. This was replaced by British government rule in 1857. Independence came to India on August 15, 1947, with the nonviolent influence of Mahatma Gandhi and the Indian National Congress. Great Britain created a Hindu India and a Moslem Pakistan because of religious tensions in the country. India remained in the British Commonwealth until January 26, 1950, when the nation became a republic.

MOTHER TERESA

Mother Teresa is a Catholic nun who, with the Missionaries of Charity, works in Calcutta's slums rescuing abandoned children, providing refuge to the dying, ministering to the sick. She won the Nobel Prize and, in spite of her fame, returned to help the poor.

Monsignor Robert Charlebois, formerly in charge of Catholic Relief Services' Eurasia Region, who knows Mother Teresa, described the essence of this special person:

"The sadness of Mother Teresa is in her eyes and in her hands. She has carried this burden of caring for the poor. She wants to heal, and the only way she can heal is to love. She doesn't see herself as an extraordinary person, she just sees an extraordinary challenge."

The simplicity of Monsignor Bob's description is really the crux of what any message about life should be. He continued:

"Mother Teresa's crusade against poverty is her crusade against people, institutions, governments, and churches who won't love. Poverty to Mother Teresa is the absence of love; it is not economics, it is not disease."

Denise McGuire, a young person working in New York as Catholic Relief Services' desk officer for Asia, the Pacific, and India, spent six months working with Mother Teresa in Calcutta. She traveled to India through a Public Service Fellowship earned after her graduation with distinction in human biology.

"I was at Stanford doing graduate work in primary health care in developing countries. I wanted to get over there myself and see what it was really like. Mother Teresa was one of my idols," Denise said, describing how she became interested in going to India.

"I was able to design my own fellowship. My local church in California had a potluck dinner and sing-along to help cover the rest of the expenses. I went over with Kate Gerwe, my roommate at college," Denise explained.

Denise's and Kate's first few days in Calcutta were the most difficult. "On the way into downtown Calcutta from the airport it was a shock. Really the worst poverty I'd ever seen. I'd never seen poverty that was so extensive, so cruel, so pervasive," Denise said. "We stayed at the YWCA in downtown Calcutta. For ninety-five cents a day we had a room and three meals." The young Americans had to scrub their little room at the YWCA to get rid of cockroaches and spider webs.

Children are the first to suffer from overcrowded, unsanitary living conditions in India's poor urban areas such as this one in Calcutta. *(UNICEF photo by S. K. Dutt)*

"The first two days were the hardest. Then when I started working with the poor, I didn't worry about my living situation, but how I could do more," Denise explained.

Denise's first encounter with Mother Teresa came at 54 A Lower Circular Road in Calcutta. "We waited a long time," Denise remembers. "When Mother Teresa came out, she put her hand on my shoulder. She has very worn and very strong hands. It's amazing how strong. She put her hand on my shoulder very firmly and kept it there the whole time she was talking with me. She looked at me while she was talking, as though there was nobody else in the room," Denise said, recapturing some of the excitement and energy of her first meeting with Mother Teresa.

"We started work at Kalighat. It is Mother Teresa's home for the dying. We worked there in the morning and at Shishu Bhavan, the children's orphanage, in the afternoon. Shishu Bhavan is not only the orphanage but the care unit for severely malnourished children," Denise explained.

"Sometimes when the Sisters went out to find abandoned children I would go out with them. Babies might be found thrown out in garbage cans. Mothers would come in and give away their children. Sometimes mothers would leave their children on the steps of the orphanage. They gave away their children, hoping the youngsters would have a chance to live. Sometimes I would see a mother come and give her baby to one of the Sisters, crying, then just run away," Denise said. This is Calcutta today, where, but for the work of Mother Teresa and the Sisters, there would be little hope for the abandoned children.

Denise and her roommate, Kate, had to do a lot of difficult work, sometimes almost more than they could bear. Mother Teresa's order operates a van with Missionaries of Charity painted on the side. They drive the van through the streets of Calcutta each day at sunrise to bring people in.

"One man was brought in who had been lying in the gutter several days," Denise said.

"They thought he was dead, but he wasn't. We put him in the

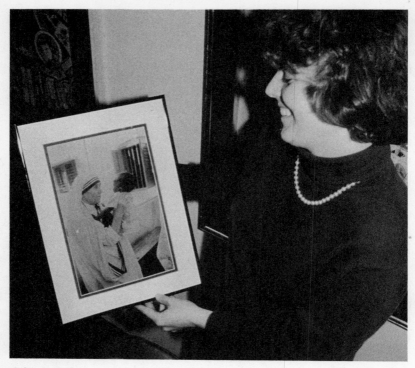

Denise McGuire in the offices of Catholic Relief Services in New York City holding a picture she took of Mother Teresa. There are many opportunities for young people to help others in need, and the experience is both rewarding and enriching. For those who have had the opportunity to work with Mother Teresa, the inspiration will stay with them always.

shower stall where the Sisters would wash arrivals from the street. This man had maggots on his feet. The Sisters poured something over him, a solution that burned, and all the maggots came out of him," Denise recalled, putting one hand to her chest as she described the ordeal.

"The next day I came back. The man was smiling. He had a hospital robe on. He wasn't any healthier, but he felt there were people who cared," Denise explained, then added something that is perhaps the most important aspect of Mother Teresa's and the Sisters' work: "If we restore human dignity before they die, we have succeeded."

Denise developed a special affection for the little children in Mother Teresa's orphanage—children who come malnourished, sick, without hope, and without a chance at life. The orphanage has had some real successes, and some of Mother Teresa's orphans have married and have even come back to the home to adopt children themselves.

What Denise took away from India may have been even more valuable than her contribution to the work among the poor.

"I felt lucky and rich. I gained more insight into the human spirit and life than from anything else I ever did in my life. I played sports in college. You think of things in your life that had so much meaning. I had an athletic scholarship. That whole time the focus was on winning, on playing in the most important games. You think there can be no greater thrill. It's nothing," Denise said.

Denise McGuire had time to grow up and play during her childhood and formative years in America; the poor people Denise saw in Calcutta had been robbed of their childhood.

Denise smiled, remembering a story about Mother Teresa that showed a person with a good sense of humor coupled with purpose. Denise once asked Mother Teresa what more she could do to help the poor. Mother Teresa answered practically, not philosophically. "Sell your shirt. You can get five dollars for it. Then buy another one for two-fifty and give the Sisters two-fifty," Mother Teresa replied, and they both laughed.

From her experience among India's desperate and dying, Denise McGuire returned home knowing that spiritual things are more meaningful than material things.

"Calcutta was one of the happiest times I've had in my life," Denise said. "There was a freedom I found in giving up things and in the simpleness of life." Among the poor she found great treasure, the riches of love.

In India, where the desperately poor have little hope, Mother Teresa and the Missionaries of Charity bring human kindness, understanding, and dignity to the desolation of death. For the children of poverty, this caring means survival.

In reporting on the state of the world's children in 1987, James P. Grant, UNICEF's executive director, described a "silent emergency" which, he said, kills well over a quarter of a million children every week. UNICEF's executive director reported: "Those children do not die of exotic diseases requiring sophisticated cures. They die in the coma of dehydration caused by diarrheal disease. They die in the distress of measles. They die in the spasms of tetanus. They die in the retchings of whooping cough. They die in the long, drawn-out process of frequent illness and poor nutrition that gradually loosens their grip on life. The deaths of these children, and the suffering of their families, cannot be framed in the viewfinder of a camera. They are therefore not news. And the world is not moved to emergency action on their behalf. But even in the last two years, infection and malnutrition have killed more young children in India and Pakistan, for example, than in all forty-six nations of Africa put together."

BANGLADESH

Wars in the name of religion have caused just as much suffering as political conflicts or territorial disputes. Years of strife between Hindus and Moslems in India were fraught with great violence.

Bangladesh is a new nation, founded in 1971. It is nearly surrounded by India but touches a corner of the Burma frontier. Bangladesh was formed from the eastern part of the former Indian state of Bengal, then known as East Pakistan. A country of 55,548 square miles with a population of 104 million people, Bangladesh is one of the poorest nations in the world.

When Bangladesh was created, strife broke out between the Pakistani army and Bangladesh insurgents. Some 10 million Hindus fled, seeking refuge in India and East Pakistan. Open warfare raged from November 1971 until the middle of December, when Pakistani troops surrendered.

War and a disastrous cyclone and tidal wave in 1970 had left the new nation ravaged. As a result of these events, many starved and more suffered malnutrition.

"Bangladesh is a success story," Monsignor Robert Charlebois

In 1983, UNICEF launched the Child Survival and Development Revolution to save the lives of millions of children in Bangladesh. *(UNICEF photo by A. Khan)*

explained, describing how local Bengali relief agencies mobilized, rising to meet the disaster.

"The local infrastructure was competent enough to deal with international donor agencies and took over to cope with the problem and distribute foreign relief aid," Monsignor Charlebois said.

By mobilizing, the new nation managed to stem mass starvation. Attention was devoted to planting the fertile soil with rice. Ample water supplies enable three harvests of rice per year. By 1981, a record crop of 14.8 million metric tons of rice was harvested, and while many are plagued with malnutrition, there is reason for optimism in Bangladesh.

CHINA

China is the third largest country in the world after Russia and Canada, occupying 3.7 million square miles. Its frontiers touch Hong Kong, Laos, and Vietnam, Korea, Burma, Bhutan, Nepal, India, Pakistan, Afghanistan, Mongolia, and Russia.

There are records documenting Chinese civilization dating back 3,500 years. Governed by a succession of dynasties, China is said to be the oldest continuous civilization on Earth.

In the nineteenth century, westerners began trading with China. Defeated by Great Britain in 1842, China was forced to concede privileges to the victor. Foreign domination and influence held sway in China until Sun Yat-sen began to unite the nation in the 1920s. Chiang Kai-shek took over in 1925.

A bitter struggle ensued between the communists under Mao Tse-tung and Chiang Kai-shek forces until the Japanese invaded and occupied the country in 1931. In 1945, after the Japanese defeat in World War II, fighting resumed between the factions in China until Chiang Kai-shek was forced to flee mainland China to Taiwan in 1949. Mao Tse-tung proclaimed the country the People's Republic of China.

The nation underwent a major social and economic revolution. Agricultural production was increased and there were many industrial advances. After Mao's death in 1976, enormous economic progress took place in a country that jumped from a feudal state into the modern world in barely two generations.

There have been grave crises in China. Throughout the nation's history famines have taken the lives of millions of people. A massive famine occurred in 1960 and 1961, which is reported to have resulted in 8 million deaths.

Government-enforced public health measures, education (the adult literacy rate is 82 percent for males and 56 percent for females), agricultural reform, flood control programs, vaccination to prevent diseases such as smallpox and cholera, and population

A student nurse weighs a child in a clinic in a Chinese village. *(United Nations Archives)*

control have all helped to eliminate hunger and abject poverty. Rice, wheat, and other grain production is up, having tripled over the last thirty years. Infant mortality in the same period was reduced from 125 per thousand live births in 1950 to around 36 today.

China is the most populous nation in the world. Feeding its one billion fifty million people in the future will require all of its agricultural resources and ocean husbandry, as well as careful planning and environmental conservation. Continued modernization and concerted effort will keep China free of the devastating famines that have plagued its history.

6

EGYPT, NORTH AFRICA, AND
THE MIDDLE EAST:
Great Squalor, Great Wealth

I saw a young child asleep on top of a pile of garbage; her parents were sprawled in the dirt along the Nile. They had no home. Flies are everywhere in droves, swarming like locusts on the food the people eat, on the food the people buy, on the people. Babies' faces, raw with pus from open sores, were covered with a myriad of flies.

NOTES MADE IN CAIRO, EGYPT,
JULY 23, 1969.

For the outsider, the Arab world holds enormous fascination. It is a place where one can see extremes: Opulence, wealth, sophistication, culture, and successful free enterprise exist next to abject poverty and squalor. Where there is poverty, there is great hardship; the social institutions designed to care for the needy seem ineffective. Often help that would make the difference between life and death is only an arm's length away, but the poor cannot reach it. Health care, good nutrition, education, and advantage often depend on a person's ability to pay.

Inshallah, an Arabic expression often heard in Egypt and other parts of the Arab world, can be roughly translated: *it is in God's hands* or *whatever God wills.* The word expresses a resignation, a fatalism that is a sort of worldview for many Moslems. Perhaps it is this worldview that explains an almost complacent acceptance of their plight, but in countries where there are the means to make life

103

better for the poor, government indifference is certainly not the will of God.

Egypt, North Africa, and the Middle East take in an amazing expanse of land where some two hundred million people live and where national differences, even regional differences within nations, make generalization impossible. While the common denominators are the inhabitants' language and religion, there are differences, nuances, in these, too. These differences, including competing religious sects and customs, create borders within borders, although for the outside world, superficial similarities seem to be universal traits.

Children are often seen leading older people blinded by diseases that could be cured or prevented with modern medicine. In Egypt, often help is nearby, but the poor cannot afford it.

EGYPT

"If there is an accident on the road, an ambulance may or may not come. It is always very long before help comes. When the injured person is taken to a hospital, a doctor may or may not be there to treat the person. There is usually long waiting before any help is administered, and that help may or may not be effective. People die for no reason. If they do not have the means to pay for it, it is their luck or not that they obtain care. This is wrong. We are talking about human life. There is help in this country, but it is beyond reach for most people." The young Egyptian pharmacy student who made this observation recently in Alexandria, Egypt, was expressing what many young people find wrong with their society.

It is not uncommon to see luxury automobiles zipping past squalor in the streets, parked near open sewers where children play. Poor children rummage through garbage, sorting the waste, looking for food.

This nation of immense cultural wealth and with a rich cultural heritage borders the Red Sea to the east and the Mediterranean in the north. It has a population of some 51 million people. While Egypt comprises 386,660 square miles in area, almost the size of California, Nevada, and Arizona combined, much of the land is arid desert, forcing the population into a narrow belt irrigated by the Nile.

Modern Egypt depends on tourist interest in the history of ancient Egypt to bring hard currency into the economy. Apart from tourism, the Egyptian economy is largely agrarian.

Egypt was drawn into the Six Day War with Israel in 1967. This conflict drained the resources of the nation, taking money away from important social reforms and diverting it to military programs. With peace, Egypt began to face the economic problems at home, including childhood diseases and malnutrition.

Official salaries in Egypt are very low, while consumer goods, especially clothing and imported items, are very expensive. A teacher in Egypt may earn forty to sixty Egyptian pounds per

Children in Alexandria, Egypt, search for food in the garbage.

month. A pair of pants in a shop may cost the equivalent of a month's wages. To feed a family, to provide shelter for that family, require all of a person's resources. In most cases it requires a lifetime of work to have enough money to obtain a suitable dwelling.

PUTTING HELP WITHIN REACH

Somewhere in the world a child dies every ten seconds of diarrheal dehydration. Approximately 3.5 million children in the world die each year from the dehydration caused by diarrhea. This condition can be cured by oral rehydration therapy cheaply and effectively, by parents at home. UNICEF estimates that though only 12 percent of the world's families are using this therapy, it has already resulted in saving 500,000 children each year.

In Egypt, where the United Nations estimates that over 100,000 children succumb each year to the dehydrating effects of diarrhea, a program educating parents in the use of oral rehydration therapy has reduced infant deaths 30 percent in Alexandria alone. A major commitment is required to educate parents in this low-cost therapy. In 1983, a campaign was begun in Egypt to put oral rehydration therapy in the hands of parents. It is now estimated that 96 percent of all Egyptian parents know about the revolutionary therapy and 82 percent have used it.

This progress prompted the chairman of Cairo University's Pediatric Medicine Department, who was Egypt's former health minister, to declare, "In my thirty-five-years practice as a pediatrician in a developing country, I have not witnessed a greater advance in medicine. One day it will be said that the end of the twentieth century has opened a new era for mankind—the post–oral rehydration-therapy era."

This good news, coupled with a commitment by Egypt's president to immunize all children, is a giant step in preventing infant mortality. Good nutrition and good health are inseparable elements in promoting human welfare.

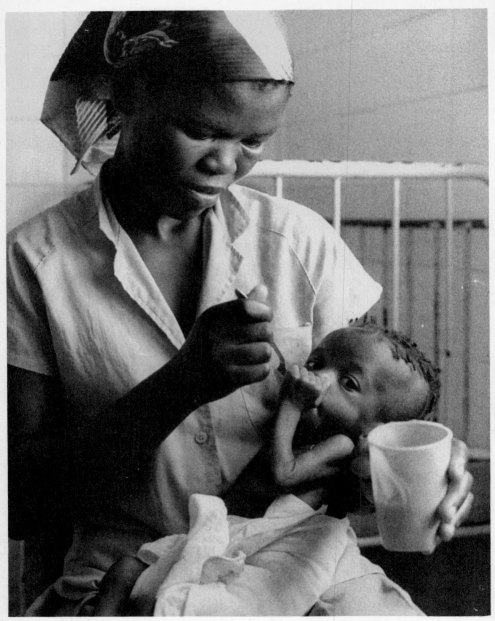

An infant suffering from dehydration is treated with oral rehydration salts in Angola. *(UNICEF photo by Maggie Murray-Lee)*

NORTH AFRICA AND THE MIDDLE EAST

Egypt is a window on North Africa and the Middle East, yet they are worlds apart. There are sheikhdoms and oil emirates where the per-capita income is the highest in the world; there are hovels where misery and suffering plumb the depths of human deprivation.

Reports coming out of strife-torn Lebanon paint a bleak picture in terms of human crisis. Displaced Palestinian refugees, factional fighting, religious warfare, and civil war have torn the little nation on the Mediterranean Sea apart. The world reeled as news reports described hostage taking, brutal murders, and terrorist attacks. What the world can only glimpse is the human toll taken on the civilian population.

Before the open hostilities, Lebanon was a modern country; Beirut was the Arab world's Paris, cosmopolitan and affluent. War and civil strife have destroyed much of the beauty of Beirut and scarred the land.

As warring factions in Beirut blockaded whole sections of the city, harried doctors reported that the people had no food. A British physician working in a cordoned-off quarter reported seeing people eating dogs, cats, and even rats to survive. A few hundred yards away, a U.N. convoy of trucks carrying food was stopped by a barrage of gunfire; one driver was killed and others wounded.

When I visited Lebanon at the onset of hostilities, my overall impression, relayed to Washington, can best be explained by describing two incidents.

We played volleyball. Some U.S. Marines, who were off-duty from their job of guarding the U.S. Embassy, and I were on one team; on the other, was a mixed group of local Lebanese men. The Lebanese argued and bickered, raised their voices, and shoved each other in the preliminary posturing, getting their team organized. They didn't get along at all, that is, until the game started and they played against us. Then the Lebanese team put aside their differences and played all out to win against the Americans.

As I was driving to the Beirut airport, our vehicle was stopped.

Civilians uprooted by the fighting gather at a relief distribution point in the Tyre area of Lebanon after a United Nations truck arrives with UNICEF supplies. *(UNICEF photo by James P. Grant)*

Young boys, perhaps eleven to thirteen years old, with automatic weapons, hand grenades attached to their makeshift uniforms, were terrorizing civilians on the road. They were stopping cars, pulling the occupants out, and in some cases setting the cars on fire. Next to them, a Lebanese army tank was stationed, its observer sitting up out of the hatch, his chin resting on his two hands, looking in the opposite direction from where the youthful, self-styled commandos were terrorizing civilians.

What I saw in these two incidents was symptomatic of the larger picture in Lebanon. Religious squabbles and differences are things the Lebanese must work out for themselves. Foreign intervention was and is fraught with peril. Lebanese aggression, as the world has seen, was shifted away from internal strife and transferred to outsiders, escalating the crisis and raising the stakes for war.

The second problem is the hands-off attitude of the government, represented by the tank commander. The government had the ability to suppress and prevent civil strife at a time when timely inter-

Symbolizing innocent victims of warfare everywhere, a young Lebanese girl stands in the rubble of what was once a neighborhood in West Beirut. *(UNICEF photo by B. Gerin)*

vention could have made a difference. For whatever reason, it chose to let it go unchecked until it was too late.

All of this describes a political condition and a war that has brought about a great deal of suffering. Innocent victims of the conflict cannot obtain food, their homes and shelters, in many cases, have been destroyed by bombardments. Children in Lebanon are suffering malnutrition and diseases caused by the breakdown of civil order and public services.

In Egypt, North Africa, and throughout the Middle East, the barrier between rich and poor is as impenetrable as any wall. Those that have wealth have health, food. Obesity is even considered a characteristic worthy of respect, for it shows the person has the means to eat well. The poor suffer greatly. It is heartbreaking to see little children eating what they can find in garbage leavings while there are ways at hand to help them.

7

LATIN AMERICA:
Very Rich, Very Poor

Across the valley, down a deep canyon, there was a village of shanties. The hovels were made of scraps of wood and discarded signboards roofed with corrugated tin and plastic sheets. Three or four little children climbed up to the bridge that crossed over their squatters' village to play, running back quickly when strangers approached. A stream, polluted with human waste and sewage, trickled through this shanty settlement in Caracas. Women were drawing water from the stream to bathe their babies and cook.

NOTES MADE IN CARACAS, VENEZUELA,
SOUTH AMERICA.

"Every gun that is made, every warship launched, every rocket fired, signifies, in the final sense, a theft from those who hunger and are not fed, those who are cold and are not clothed. This world in arms is not spending money alone. It is spending the sweat of its laborers, the genius of its scientists, the hopes of its children. . . . This is not a way of life at all, in any true sense. Under the cloud of threatening war, it is humanity hanging from a cross of iron." It wasn't a pacifist who made this declaration, rather it was the man who commanded all Allied forces in World War II.

Dwight D. Eisenhower's declaration that guns steal food from the hungry has application all over the world; no place is it more apparent than in Latin America today.

Latin America generally describes the vast continent from Mexico to the tip of South America. Islands in the Caribbean basin are

113

In Rio de Janeiro, families of street children depend on them as their only means of support. *(UNICEF photo by William Hetzer)*

included in the Latin America area by international organizations responsible for administering aid in the region. Mexico, Central and South America, and the Caribbean make up a vast geographic sphere where more than 415 million people live.

The term Latin America is derived from the fact that most people in the region speak Spanish, though Brazil, a nation of 143.3 million people, where Portuguese is spoken, is a notable exception. Caribbean islanders speak a variety of languages, depending on early colonial influence, be it English, French, Dutch, or Spanish, as well as their own dialects. No nation in the Americas is the same and no generalization is applicable, but there are common denominators: poverty, childhood malnutrition, and disease.

Volatile political systems, social and economic crises, warfare, turmoil, and internal strife have left many Latin American countries unstable. In spite of these problems, national and international programs to help alleviate hunger and the causes of disease have made progress.

UNICEF has been involved in Latin America and the Caribbean for many years, working in the fields of health, education, and nutrition and trying to cope with the vast problems of infant mortality, childhood diseases, and malnutrition. Latin America is a place of stark contrasts. One can see great wealth and the conveniences of modern society and great poverty with people living in squalor.

Describing its work since 1948, when the international organization began programs in the Americas, UNICEF reported: "Meaningful statistics notwithstanding, and even given the general availability of food, UNICEF, from its earliest days, identified child malnutrition as a serious problem in the Americas."

UNICEF's medical workers, who conducted studies throughout Latin America, found that in rural areas, where there was land to grow food, nutritional deficiency diseases were "due more to a lack of parental understanding of the nutritional values of foods and their relation to health, while in the cities, the frequent cause was poverty, which resulted in the children being underfed." UNICEF research-

A child carries the family water supply in a shanty town of Bogotá, Colombia. *(UNICEF photo by Horst Cerni)*

ers also found that milk shortages were affecting child health, causing protein deficiencies.

Many of the regional organizations, such as the Organization of
American States (OAS), worked closely with UNICEF and the
World Health Organization (WHO) to implement inoculation programs against childhood diseases. Programs were undertaken to improve education, which is at the root of poverty and of poor health
and nutrition. For example, in Peru, communities built centers
called "Wawa Wasi" (House of the Child). They are day-care centers staffed by volunteers to stimulate and educate young children.

Many Latin American governments are faced with huge international debts and resulting staggering interest payments. For example, in 1982, the external debt of Latin American nations amounted
to 300 billion dollars, double what it was in 1979. Inflation rose, so
that in 1984, the level of inflation was 165.3 percent for the region.
What all this complicated international economic jargon means for
the poor is that Latin American countries have been forced to cut
back on aid programs. And, because of inflation, the money people
earn allows them to buy less food.

On top of recent economic hard times, Latin America has been
rocked with natural disasters: earthquakes in Chile and Mexico,
volcanoes and mud slides in Colombia, flooding in Argentina, be-
sides the wars in many countries. While there has been great change,
there has been no change, for everywhere in the Americas the crisis
of the poor continues: Their suffering is directly related to warfare
and strife.

UNICEF launched important programs in the Americas. There
were projects to monitor children's growth and weight to help diag-
nose malnutrition. Oral rehydration therapy packets and information were given to parents to teach them how to prevent dehydration
when a child suffers diarrhea. Campaigns were begun to encourage
breast-feeding of infants, alerting mothers to vitamin deficiencies
that often occur when using bottled or powdered milk, and dangers
inherent in preparing the milk with unsanitary water. Immunization
programs to prevent childhood killer diseases such as measles, diph-

UNICEF supplies food to victim of an earthquake in El Salvador. *(UNICEF photo by Dennis Budd Gray)*

theria, tuberculosis, polio, tetanus, and whooping cough were instituted.

In the summer of 1984, a crusade was launched in Colombia to vaccinate children. The entire nation was mobilized by national health organizations, volunteers, and public officials. When the campaign was over, more than 800,000 children had received their inoculations, an important step for child survival.

Government and warring El Salvador guerrilla forces observed a truce that enabled 20,000 health workers and trained volunteers to inoculate children at temporary vaccination posts. *(UNICEF photo by Dennis Budd Gray)*

Even in the midst of the terrible war in El Salvador, UNICEF, the World Health Organization, and the Pan American Health Organization were able to negotiate three "days of tranquility," when government forces and guerrillas joined with the Catholic Church and the Red Cross to enforce a temporary cease-fire so that 250,000 children could be inoculated against the major diseases that can be prevented with modern vaccines.

The extraordinary truce and cooperation among the forces of war in strife-torn El Salvador, prompted James Grant, UNICEF's executive director, to declare, that this was "The first time on record a country-wide conflict gave way to a health intervention for saving the lives of thousands of children."

Discussing the problems in the region, Teresa Albanez, UNICEF's regional director for Latin America and the Caribbean, said that "approximately forty percent of the population of the region is living under the critical line of poverty." She pointed out that many of the poor in this group are suffering the effects of malnutrition.

"What we have observed, what has been demonstrated by studies in Latin America in recent years, tends to show an aggravation of malnutrition levels in certain populations," Teresa Albanez explained. "In Brazil, for example, the number of children with low weight levels is increasing. Studies made in preschool children aged from three to six years indicates nineteen percent of the children in Latin America suffer from malnutrition," UNICEF's regional director added.

"In Latin America, we see a different degree of malnutrition, not starvation and hunger, only exceptionally where there is a drought or disaster. Malnutrition is on the increase," said Kul Gautam, UNICEF's chief of the Americas section at U.N. headquarters in New York.

"Basically it is a vicious cycle. Malnutrition alone may not kill the child, but infections that complicate malnutrition, measles and diarrhea account for high mortality in children," Kul Gautam added.

"This malnutrition is due to two factors," Teresa Albanez explained. "Of course insufficient food intake is one factor. Second is the environmental situation and poor hygiene in the population.

"The food intake is not enough and with poor hygiene, what the people eat is not absorbed properly. There are many intestinal and parasitic diseases," Teresa said. "A child in the Latin American region, between birth and two years old, has between two and seven-tenths to ten and more diarrhea episodes in a year's span of time. Each episode means that whatever the child has eaten is expelled with diarrhea.

"On the growth chart, we can see the child has difficulty every time there is an episode of diarrhea, which means there is a weight loss." Teresa Albanez then touched on the heart of the crisis for the poor in Latin America: "The problem of malnutrition in the region is silent. The problem is invisible. The child does not have the appearance of a starved child, but there is a loss [of size and general health] because of malnutrition."

"That is one of the dilemmas. There is not a net deficit of food in Latin America, but there is a need in some parts of many of the countries in the region," Kul Gautam said. "If you look back over the statistics for the past ten years, the per capita incomes are the same or lower today. There is a net deterioration. Where you have a deterioration in the economy, it is usually the poor, the women and children who suffer the effects," Kul added.

Teresa Albanez noted that since inflation is rampant, people's buying power is affected. "The power to buy food is less. What we see, with sadness, is the adjustment in the family. It is applied to the dining table. People go to work, so they have to pay transportation, they have to pay for other things, therefore they eat less and there is less quality to their food. The first to eat less are women and girls. The father eats first, whether he is employed or not. The last to eat is the mother, and probably she is pregnant," Teresa explained.

Kul Gautam, a native of Nepal, who has worked with UNICEF for fourteen years in Southeast Asia, Cambodia, Laos, Indonesia, and most recently in Haiti before becoming chief of the Americas section, offered his further observations of the problems. "Let me tell you, malnutrition is becoming a growing concern for UNICEF and in the countries of Latin America. We are strengthening our actions for child survival and child development," Kul said, pointing out many of UNICEF's successes in the field of disease prevention, education, and nutrition.

Many of the problems in the region covered by UNICEF's Latin America bureau seem insurmountable. "Take one example," Kul

Working children in Brazil. This is often their only way to survive. *(UNICEF photo by Shelley Rotner)*

Gautam said. "Haiti, an island in the Caribbean covered by our region, at the beginning of this century was seventy percent covered with forests. Today there is only seven percent forest. The rest was destroyed for firewood and building. Haiti may be an Ethiopia in the making. Haiti has every conceivable problem. Over seventy percent of the children in Haiti are malnourished, over thirty percent are badly malnourished—second degree malnourishment we call it," Kul said, describing an island nation where overpopulation has strained the natural resources and limited the amount of food available to feed the people.

While there is a new government in Haiti, it is evident that Kul

Gautam is realistic when he says, "We hope things will change for the better, but it will not happen overnight."

Kul's observation can be applied to all of Latin America, where poverty has created a whole generation of street children who live by their wits. Many of them are without families, suffering in urban slums, living on the streets.

In Latin America today, there is extreme wealth. In many countries there is an overabundance of food, so much food that many of the nations are major exporters. For the poor, much of that wealth belongs to another world, a world that they can see but never touch. Opulence and wealth in Latin America is often in the hands of a few powerful families, in countries where power is maintained by force. Huge external debts, which have created inflation and hard economic times, have often been caused by spending for military arms. It is a vicious cycle, which makes the words of the late Allied commander in World War II, America's thirty-fourth president, relevant:

"Every gun that is made, every warship launched, every rocket fired, signifies, in the final sense, a theft from those who hunger and are not fed," Dwight D. Eisenhower said. He could very well have been describing the dilemma in Latin America today.

8

THE UNITED STATES:
"L'Amerique!"

The little girl ran with outstretched arms, eyes wide, hands open, a look of anticipation on her face. The kids helping out in the storefront soup kitchen handed the child a tray of food. The child took the tray and ran back through the dimly lit hallway to rejoin her mother and little brothers outside in the rain. Hunger in America is very real. It is saddest when children do not get enough to eat or are not fed nourishing meals.

NOTES MADE IN HARLEM, NEW YORK,
SOUP KITCHEN, APRIL 18, 1987.

From my office window I see three men asleep on the street above power company steam tunnels. It is below freezing outside. These homeless men have made the steam tunnel grates their home. Earlier I passed by and saw them cooking directly over a steam-drain covering, using the heat to warm what they have scavenged from the fish market leavings.

These homeless men wear ragged clothes, black with dirt and grease; they sleep rolled up in old rags, on cardboard boxes, plastic bags, and scraps of cloth rescued from garbage. By nightfall the temperature drops to fifteen degrees, seeming even colder with the wind. As I watch, a police car stops, some order is given, and the three derelicts pick up their rags and move around the corner. They will come back once the police patrol leaves; they cannot survive in this cold winter away from the steam grates.

This is New York, but it is the same everywhere in America's big

124

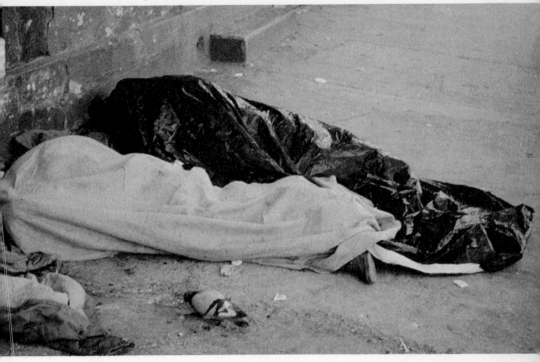

These homeless men live on the street in lower Manhattan, New York. They eat what they can rummage from the leavings of the fish market and cook their food on the steam tunnels that run beneath the pavement, where they sleep to survive freezing winter weather.

cities. Why can't we cope with the homeless in America? It cannot be said that they are less wretched than the poor of Calcutta's slums. At least the temperature in India is kinder, although governmental indifference and the bureaucratic inability to solve the problem is just as insidious.

L'Amerique! It is a French pop word for the life-style in the land of plenty. In fact, America is more than a country or a life-style; it represents an ideal—a hope for millions of oppressed people everywhere in the world. America is a place of freedom, a place where the importance of human dignity is a national credo. To fulfill its destiny, America must remain true to this national ideal, a place where all people are afforded dignity of the human spirit.

BROTHER, CAN YOU SPARE A DIME?

"You weren't born in the Great Depression. I remember how it was," parents or grandparents might say, confronting their young people with recollections of hard times in America. The refrain of the sad tune "Brother, Can You Spare a Dime?" remains a poignant chronicle of hardships during the Great Depression in the United States. The song recalls a period in American history when many people were out of work and had to stand on lines for free food. The economic turmoil of 1929 and the early thirties brought home to many Americans the desperation of being poor, without the means to buy food and support a family.

It is important to remember lessons of the Great Depression, for even in a modern society with all of the safeguards of government programs, economic chaos, natural disaster, war, and disruption of peoples' lives can lead quickly to tragedy.

There are pockets of poverty in America, where depressed economies in urban and rural environments have left an impact on people. Cases of malnourished children living in poverty are reported throughout the United States, from the rural south to industrialized northern cities.

Poverty and ignorance account for the fact that children are brought up without proper food and health care. As we have seen in some parts of the world, help is just an arm's length away, although the poor cannot reach it. There are places in America today with similar needs. In the United States, help is available to all, regardless of their ability to pay for it. But in many cases, ignorance, poor attitudes, mental illness, or injustice puts that help beyond the reach of those in need.

No nation can afford to be smug about the relative well-being of its citizens. In the United States, statistics reveal that households below the poverty level are on the rise. In New York City, the number of children living in poverty has increased from 25 to 40 percent of all the city's children. In 1969, children living in poverty in the United States amounted to 14 percent of the population; that figure rose to 22 percent in 1985.

Kids grow up in the South Bronx, in New York City, playing among garbage, often living in burned-out shells of tenements, eating what they can scavenge. These two children play amid debris-littered tenements. America's dream has been tarnished by neglect.

A 1986 report by the Physician Task Force on Hunger in America, listed 150 counties as the worst hunger zones. The counties listed were those where "large numbers of citizens experience hunger and high risk of nutritional deprivation." The report assessed the greatest need and attempted to identify a gap in the national food stamp assistance program, which provides the poor with free coupons to buy food in supermarkets and food stores. The Task Force identified 716 counties in the United States where 20 percent or more of the population fell below the poverty level established in 1979. The 150 counties judged by the Task Force to be "hunger counties" were those among the 716 with the lowest 1984 food stamp participation.

The Task Force report, considered controversial and challenged by local and national authorities on the basis of the methods used, is an important indication of concern about the problem of hunger in America.

The U.S. General Accounting Office (GAO), the auditing arm of Congress, reported in 1983: "During the recent serious recession, when unemployment rates throughout the country were at their highest levels in decades, an increasing number of Americans were seeking food assistance." What the GAO found was that "an official national 'hunger count' does not exist," and "no one knows precisely how many Americans are going hungry or how many are malnourished." The GAO found, however, that the institutions providing emergency food assistance were reporting significant increases over past years.

The government reported that federal funding for food assistance programs was 17.8 billion dollars in 1983 and 16.6 billion dollars in 1984. Many private organizations established food banks to help the poor, using surplus food either from U.S. Department of Agriculture surplus government supplies or edible food donated by the private sector that otherwise would be wasted.

There are many federal, state, and local welfare programs to aid the poor in America. Of course there are abuses in these programs.

Many people receive public assistance, food stamps to buy food in markets, rent allowances, free health care, and other free services who may not deserve these benefits. Scandals appear in the press and rampant fraud is everywhere in the system of public assistance and welfare. It is also true that many deserving people are not reached by the system. As a result, many children fall through the cracks of systematic safeguards designed to prevent hunger, malnutrition, and poor health care in America. All of this presents important questions that must be answered if we are to be responsive to the needs of all Americans.

We see people with obvious mental health problems and drug or alcohol addicts sleeping in the streets and in public waiting rooms and train stations. Many people beg, and some have taken to the streets, homeless, without shelter, exposed to the elements, as were the men described at the beginning of this chapter.

Nowhere is the dilemma more apparent than in many large cities. In New York, at the exit of the United Nations garage, homeless camp out, their makeshift cardboard homes set over underground steam tunnels for warmth in subfreezing winter temperatures. They suffer and are hungry in the shadow of the headquarters of the institution established to alleviate suffering around the world.

This image is symbolic of society's failure to cope with a pressing problem: a homeless person, stretched out on the ground, a cardboard box for shelter, the United Nations headquarters as neighbor.

The U.S. Congress, in 1987, appropriated 500 million dollars to help the homeless. In a nation where major cities are wracked with scandal as politicians and their cohorts rip off the system for personal profit, one wonders how much of this help will actually reach the needy; whether programs, once implemented, will be run competently, without waste and abuse. These are important issues and the track record in the United States is poor. Without integrity, programs designed to help the poor will be discredited, eventually eliminated, and new programs to aid the needy discouraged.

Homeless camp out in the shadow of the United Nations headquarters building in New York City. People go hungry near home, often in front of the very eyes of world leaders who are responsible for famine relief.

RESURRECTION HOUSE

Governmental systems and programs to alleviate hunger are important. More important are people and their dedication to helping others, doing what they do because they see a need and, with generous heart, respond.

Resurrection House is a family service center in Harlem, New York. It operates out of a frame house in a row of tenements in one of the city's poorest neighborhoods. It is a tough neighborhood, with hard streets and hard poverty, burned-out buildings, drug and alcohol addiction, and crime. Resurrection House is in the center of the reality of urban poverty in America today. Yet in the midst of almost insurmountable problems, a small staff and volunteer workers give out free food and clothing, a moment of kindness, goodwill, and a little hope.

Young people from suburban churches help. The kids bring food and work in the kitchen Saturdays, making salads and preparing hot meals to feed a steady stream of adults and children.

"The work is about feeding poor people," Vivian Dixon, the outwardly tough director of Resurrection House said. "We have a soup kitchen open on Saturday, and a pantry open five days a week. We also offer advice on health, help make people aware of their benefits, even make telephone calls for them," Vivian explained, while mopping the linoleum floor clean of footprints, directing the volunteers, and working in the kitchen to get the food ready.

"We go to the meetings to make our legislators aware of hunger, as if they don't know," Vivian declared. "We write petitions. It's also just being here for people in the community. Sometimes they don't need material things, just a place to talk," Vivian said, describing Resurrection House, then in the next breath ordering young volunteers Adam and Chris Choi and Willie Dering to wash their hands. These young volunteers from the Scarsdale Community Baptist Church were driven to Harlem by Ruth Spillman and Janet Spence, to help prepare the meals. When they came back from the washroom, Vivian and Ruth set them to work grating carrots and preparing fresh salad in a huge bowl.

"Use the grater like this," Vivian said with authority, taking a carrot from one of the boys whose fingers were in jeopardy. "You know, we don't serve human meat here," Vivian added with a wonderful laugh, as she left the kids and went back to attend to the dozens of chores around the kitchen that had to be done before the two hundred plates could be filled with food.

"In the pantry we give out food staples. We also serve hot breakfasts two days a week. Our intake sheet shows that the people come here without breakfast. We asked them when they last ate. Most responded, the night before. So we try to give them a hot meal while they are waiting for the food," Vivian explained.

The young people from the Scarsdale Community Baptist Church had to take a lesson from Resurrection House Director Vivian Dixon about how to use the carrot grater to prevent "human meat" from getting into the salad. Resurrection House tries to offer a balanced diet so that the children get at least one hot meal with fresh salad and vegetables.

Free canned goods and other food staples distributed at the Resurrection House pantry and the hot meals they serve only supplement other forms of assistance. "Most of the people in our area are on some form of assistance: welfare, food stamps. They say New York gives out the biggest allotment for welfare, but most of that, three-quarters of that, goes for rent. Let's say a family of four gets $150 worth of food stamps, divide that by four for a month," Vivian said, describing the need that remains over what government assistance programs provide.

"I don't see anyone starving," Vivian said. "I do see malnutrition. They can't get proper food. I've seen mothers who buy a bag of popcorn and soda or potato chips for breakfast. The kids reach into the bag of popcorn and get filled up. A healthy breakfast costs too much and has to be prepared. They are not starved, but they are not properly fed," she added.

For the meals prepared in the Resurrection House kitchen, the staff and volunteer church workers try to offer nutritious servings with fresh salad, a hot main dish, fruit, bread, and dessert.

"Most of our food for the kitchen comes from government sources. We get food from the Human Resources Administration and Emergency Food Program. There is also the federal government's Surplus Food Program. We have to pay a dollar fifty per case for that, not for the food but for the storage. We also get donations from churches, like the Scarsdale Community Baptist Church and others, that send money and food," Vivian explained.

Resurrection House operates rent-free out of a converted frame house that serves as a private school called the Children's Storefront during the week. "The idea for Resurrection House came from the Dominican Sisters. It was really a follow-up for patients. They did social work as well as providing health care. The only way to administer health care was to give the people a healthy environment," Vivian explained.

"It was called the Life Center then. My aunt was working for them. At the time, I was a bookkeeper in a store. The store was destroyed by vandals, and I lost my job. That's how I started working

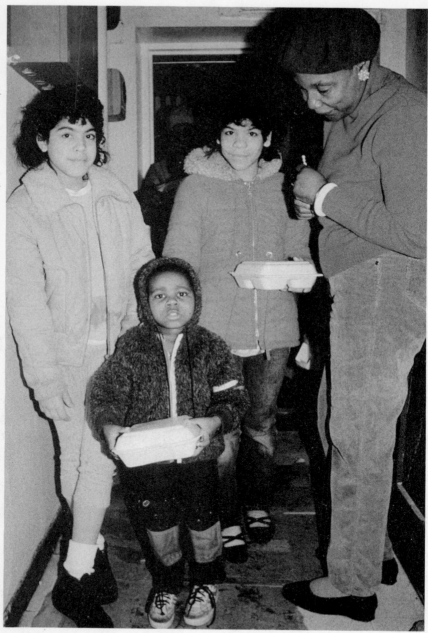

Vivian Dixon, Director of Resurrection House, looks on as a child receives a hot meal from volunteers Yahaira and Guemara Cantero.

here. It was Easter 1979 when we moved to this building. We felt we were rising from the ashes, so we called it Resurrection House," the director said.

"It's good for the young people. They don't get that much money from welfare. Here they can get hot food for free," said Marge Brown, who has been working at Resurrection House for six years.

"I know where I come from. When my kids were little and we needed help, there was nobody to give us clothing and hot meals. I get here at five o'clock in the morning. I don't get tired. I like this work. You see, it's very important," Marge emphasized. "Sometimes the line is all the way down the block, there are so many waiting for food," she added.

Willie Deering, Chris and Adam Choi serve up hot food for hungry people under the watchful eye of Resurrection House Director Vivian Dixon.

"We never refuse anyone," Vivian Dixon said, declaring, "If you're poor and in need, you're in need. Anyone that's going to stand outside there in the rain waiting for food is in need," she added emphatically, motioning to the line of people waiting outside on the rain-soaked street for the soup kitchen to open.

As the last of the people picked up their Styrofoam trays of food, two young helpers, sisters Yahaira and Guemara Cantero, handed them cups of juice and the last slices from the bags of day-old, donated bread. The food supply was almost gone.

Marge Brown and sisters Yahaira and Guemara Cantero distribute day-old bread to poor people in the Harlem community.

"Would you like to use these doughnuts?" asked Willie Dering, one of the young volunteers helping dish out the food, offering the box he had brought for his lunch. The other kids gave up what was left of their lunches as well, so that even the last of the people waiting for food went away with something.

"We have poverty in Harlem for a lot of reasons: drugs, ignorance, lack of education. I don't even have other friends anymore," Vivian Dixon said, the rough exterior melting away, showing the generosity of her kind heart. "These people are my friends. It breaks my heart," the director of Resurrection House said quietly as the group of suburban young people and their adult leaders filed out to go home, a glimmer of sunshine trying to push through the rain, brightening 127th Street for a moment.

"It was good, a good thing," Chris Choi said on the ride back to Scarsdale, only a half hour from the other world he and the other young people had just visited.

Young people from the Scarsdale Community Baptist Church with their adult leaders and the directors of Resurrection House in Harlem, New York, after serving meals to the hungry.

There are community kitchens and pantries like Resurrection House in many parts of the United States. If there is a need, then the idea is easy to implement. Merchants, restaurants, bakeries, and supermarkets are often willing to donate food that would otherwise be sold cheaply as surplus (like day-old bread and cakes) or wasted. Food drives at churches and community centers can also provide staples to supply emergency food pantries.

All it takes is a willingness to get involved. Volunteer programs can be organized through scouting, youth clubs, houses of worship, and schools. Young people, pooling their efforts to help others, find it is not only satisfying, but it opens educational horizons, molding good future citizens.

Vivian Dixon's motto at Resurrection House is "None of us is as smart as all of us." It describes the importance of people working together to help others in need.

Need does not have to be far away in Africa or Cambodia. Often there are people in need not more than a half hour from home. In America, hunger and poverty exist. They can be eliminated if we care enough to help. For we are all human beings together.

Bibliography and Other Sources

A bibliography is really the beginning, not the end of a book. For the reader concerned with problems of world hunger, material listed here will provide resources for further study. The best way to begin research is to have a talk with your local reference librarian. New indexing tools are being developed for libraries taking advantage of computer technology. These computer files help key into current literature, and your reference librarian will know about these tools and can help you use them. A topic as broad as world hunger, in the forefront of current events as disasters are reported, is covered in magazines, periodicals, and newspapers, often with investigative reports that provide up-to-the-minute information. Books can provide in-depth reports and will give historical perspective.

Ways to Find Articles in Magazines and Periodicals
INFOTRAC—This is a computerized subject index of magazine articles developed by Information Access Co., 11 Davis Dr., Belmont, CA 94002. They have toll free numbers to call: 800-227-8431; in California, 800-626-9935. INFOTRAC II contains computerized bibliographical information indexing some 400 magazines and periodicals by subject, updated monthly with a new compact disc. Some libraries have this computer system, which enables a researcher to type in a key word, *hunger,* for example, and view a screen display of articles published over the last four years or so. Developing a key word list is very helpful. A researcher may wish to key in *famine* or *food* or use other key words to bring up lists of articles stored in INFOTRAC. Many libraries have equipped their system with a

139

printer, so that "hard copy" lists of the articles stored can be generated from the system. Some libraries also subscribe to the larger INFOTRAC system that gives bibliographical citations and indexes some 900 journals and periodicals.

Magazine Index—This is an alphabetical subject index on film produced by the same company that developed INFOTRAC. It is used by many libraries. The system requires a researcher to use key words to identify the subjects being searched. *Magazine Index* lists articles for the last four years.

The Reader's Guide to Periodical Literature—*The Reader's Guide* is an index of magazine articles that goes much further back in time (the first volume was published in 1900), listing articles on any given subject. It is published by the H.W. Wilson Co., and, with their updates, is about two months behind current material.

The Reader's Guide Abstracts—This is a microfiche alphabetical abstract of articles by subject and author. There is a two to three month lag between the last microfiche entry and current materials. The abstracts currently take in an eighteen-month period.

The New York Times Index—This regularly updated index lists articles that have appeared in the *New York Times.* Key words such as *food, famine, Ethiopia,* for example, will produce a long listing of articles. Most libraries maintain microfilm copies of the *New York Times.* Entries help establish dates that can be checked in other newspapers.

Editorial Research Reports—These reports are published by *Congressional Quarterly.* Every week a different topic is covered. They provide looseleaf booklets on the Third World, energy, technology, and other subjects.

Organizations

Some international, governmental, and private organizations will be happy to provide copies of their reports upon request. While we cannot list all worthwhile organizations, here are some that can provide reports and information about hunger:

United States General Accounting Office (GAO)—GAO is the auditing arm of Congress. It conducts program reviews on its own and as a result of specific requests from members of Congress. GAO has issued a number of reports about hunger, and they may be obtained free of charge by writing:

U.S. General Accounting Office, Document Handling and Information Services Facility
PO Box 6015
Gaithersburg, MD 20760
Telephone: 202-275-6241

Some of the GAO report titles include:

Public and Private Efforts to Feed America's Poor

Hunger Counties—Methodological Review of a Report by the Physician Task Force on Hunger

Food Inventories—Inventory Management of Federally Owned and Donated Surplus Foods

Financial and Management Improvements Needed in the Food for Development Program

AID Recognizes the Need to Improve the Foreign Economic Assistance Planning and Programming Process

Can More Be Done to Assist Sahelian Governments to Plan and Manage Their Economic Development?

Catholic Relief Services (CRS) publishes reports about their work along with annual summaries of their activities in all developing countries. The CRS annual report is available by writing their headquarters in New York. CRS, like many denominational and church programs, operates many programs to help relieve hunger around the world. They are receptive to individuals and groups wishing to help raise funds for any of their worthwhile programs and projects to supply food for the hungry.

Catholic Relief Services
World Headquarters
1011 First Ave.
New York, NY 10022
Telephone: 212-838-4700

The Agency for International Development (AID) administers America's overseas foreign assistance programs and has an office equipped to respond to disasters. AID publishes reports about their work in the area of famine relief. Further information may be obtained by writing AID headquarters in Washington.

The Agency for International Development
U.S. Department of State
Washington, D.C. 20523

United Nations Children's Fund (UNICEF) has saved many from starvation. There is a United States Committee for UNICEF located at 331 East 38th Street, New York, New York 10016, telephone 212-686-5522, which can guide volunteer efforts to help UNICEF. UNICEF offices at the United Nations Building in New York maintain a Division of Information and Public Affairs at 3 United Nations Plaza, New York, NY 10017. Helpful publications that may be obtained by writing UNICEF include:

The State of the World's Children—This is an important report, which should be consulted first as a reference source about hunger and health problems worldwide.

Children on the Front Line (concerns problems in Southern Africa)

UNICEF Annual Report

UNICEF in the Americas for the Children of Three Decades

One Step for Women a Mile in Development

The State of the World's Children: A Statistical Picture

In addition to specific reports, UNICEF publishes regular news features about their work in various areas. UNICEF reports are updated regularly. Ask for the most recent issue.

Resurrection House is a Harlem food distribution center. Volunteer programs anywhere there may be a need may want to write the directors for information or to offer help.
Resurrection House
2057 Fifth Ave.
New York, NY 10035
Telephone: 212-348-3535

Food and Agriculture Organization (FAO) publishes many documents relating to agriculture, animals, conservation, fisheries, food, nutrition, etc. FAO publications are distributed by:
BERNAN-UNIPUB
4611-F Assembly Dr.
Lanham, MD 20706-4391
Toll free telephone: 800-233-0506 or 301-459-7666
A card or free telephone call to BERNAN-UNIPUB requesting their catalog of FAO publications will be useful for researching specific topics in the areas of food and nutrition.

United Nations Disaster Relief Organization (UNDRO) publishes documents about disaster. *UNDRO in Africa When Disaster Strikes,* along with their other reports and monthly bulletins, are useful research tools.
UNDRO Liason Office
United Nations Room S-2935
United Nations, New York, NY 10017

Books

Egan, Eileen. *Such a Vision of the Street: Mother Teresa—The Spirit and the Work.* Garden City, NY: Doubleday & Co., 1985.

Ending Hunger: An Idea Whose Time Has Come. New York: Praeger Publishers, 1985.

Fine, John Christopher. *Oceans In Peril.* New York: Atheneum, 1987.

Kent, George. *The Political Economy of Hunger: The Silent Holocaust.* New York: Praeger, 1984.

Lappé, Frances Moore. *World Hunger: Twelve Myths.* New York: Grove Press, 1986.

Leinwand, Gerald. *Hunger and Malnutrition in America.* New York: Watts, 1985.

Physician Task Force on Hunger in America. *The Growing Epidemic.* Connecticut: Wesleyan University Press, distributed by Harper & Row, 1985.

Serrou, Robert. *Teresa of Calcutta: a Pictorial Biography.* New York: McGraw Hill, 1980.

Spiegelman, Judith M. *We Are the Children.* New York: Atlantic Monthly Press, 1986.

Teresa, Mother. *My Life for the Poor.* San Francisco: Harper & Row, 1985.

Teresa, Mother, and Lee, Betsy. *Mother Teresa: Caring For All God's Children.* Minneapolis: Dillon Press, 1981.

U.S. Presidential Commission on World Hunger. *Technical Papers.* The Presidential Commission on World Hunger, 1980.

INDEX

145